"The word *Myth* often refers either to a widespread falsehood or to an ancient collection of stories about gods and heroes. Charlie Starr delves more deeply into the term, offering surprising new insights into fiction, faith, gender, and even human nature itself. With his thorough research and readable prose, Starr lays a solid foundation for novice readers of Lewis (and Tolkien) and provides fresh illumination even for lifelong readers of Lewis and his friends."—**David C. Downing**, codirector (with his wife Crystal) of the Marion E. Wade Center, Wheaton College, and author of six books on C. S. Lewis and the Inklings

"*The Faun's Bookshelf* explores one of the most important aspects of Lewis studies: how Lewis's deep and abiding affection for myth undergirds, informs, and enriches both his fiction and poetry. Charlie Starr's approach is inviting, conversational, and winsome. Readers will come away with a thorough understanding of Lewis's mythic vision—including the mythic sources that influenced him and how Lewis used them in his own work. This book is long overdue and a welcome addition to Lewis studies."—**Don W. King**, author of *C. S. Lewis Poet: The Legacy of His Poetic Impulse* and editor of *The Collected Poems of C. S. Lewis: A Critical Edition*

"This is a delightful book, at once erudite and accessible, that asks just the right questions about Lewis and myth and that answers them by searching in nooks and crannies of the Lewis corpus that have too often been overlooked."—**Louis Markos**, professor of English and scholar in residence, Houston Baptist University; author of *On the Shoulders of Hobbits: The Road to Virtue with Tolkien and Lewis*

"Students of C. S. Lewis's thought know that the phrase 'myth become fact' is central to his conversion, to his theology, and to the whole way his mind worked. In *The Faun's Bookshelf*, Charlie Starr rings the changes on that phrase to show that it is more central than we could have guessed—to everything mentioned above and to Lewis's imagination, his art, and the meaning of his stories as well. Lewis comes alive as a theorist and a practitioner of myth in a book that could deservedly be added to Mr. Tumnus's library. I am delighted to have added it to mine."—**Donald T. Williams**, R. A. Forrest Scholar at Toccoa Falls College and author of *Deeper Magic: The Theology behind the Writings of C. S. Lewis*

"Starr teaches us how and why myth matters, but he also entertains—even amuses—us while doing so. He guides us to that intersection of the whimsical, the profound, and the sacred. Wouldn't Lewis (Tolkien, too) be delighted? Seldom do I see a scholarly book this creative and readable."—**Carolyn Curtis**, coeditor of *Women and C.S. Lewis: What His Life and Literature Reveal for Today's Culture*

"*The Faun's Bookshelf* is a fascinating exploration of the mythological underpinnings present in C. S. Lewis's fictional worlds. It gives the reader a better understanding of the blend of myths used to 'sing' Narnia into existence, and reminds us of the abiding Truth in old legends. Charlie Starr's exceptional work provides us with a refreshing lens to, once again, approach and appreciate Lewis's marvelous fiction. I read this book with great delight!"—**Crystal Hurd**, author of *Thirty Days with C.S. Lewis: A Women's Devotional* and review editor for *Sehnsucht: The C. S. Lewis Journal*

"A clever premise beautifully executed. Scrutinizing the books on Mr. Tumnus's bookshelf helps us understand not only the mythic world of Narnia but our own world as well. Grab a cup of tea then settle in for a good 'conversation' with Charlie Starr. This masterfully crafted book will leave you affirmed, challenged, and grateful for the visit."—**Steven A. Beebe**, Regents' and University Distinguished Professor of Communication Studies, Texas State University

"Charlie Starr's mastery of the essays written by C. S. Lewis is particularly impressive. Lewis readers will discover here how long-cherished passages can be paired with little-known extracts to yield fresh insights regarding myth and meaning. The bookshelf of Mr. Tumnus will never appear quite the same again. Over the titles Lucy found there we must now all linger."—**Bruce R. Johnson**, general editor of *Sehnsucht: The C. S. Lewis Journal*

"Starr's thoughtful consideration of a seemingly trivial witticism in the first Narnian chronicle has led to this book, the most comprehensive study yet of what myth meant to Lewis and what it can mean to us. Citations drawn from the whole range of Lewis's writings—including some only recently discovered—are woven into a tapestry given substance by Starr's expert understanding of Lewis's views on imagination, meaning, and truth. Newcomers to Lewis will find this book accessible, with its winsome style developed over years of classroom teaching; seasoned scholars will find challenging new insights."—**Charles Huttar**, author of numerous studies of the Inklings, including *Word and Story in C. S. Lewis* (coeditor) and *Imagination and the Spirit* (editor)

"*The Faun's Bookshelf* is a delightful read. In an engaging way Charlie Starr provides the necessary background about what myth means for Lewis and helps all readers understand more fully why myth matters!"—**William O'Flaherty**, author of *The Misquotable C.S. Lewis* and creator of EssentialCSLewis.com

"Charlie Starr's insightful and readable explanation of why myth matters is the most illuminating, interesting, and important book on myth and mythopoeia that I am aware of."—**Peter J. Schakel**, author of *The Way into Narnia* and *Imagination and the Arts in C. S. Lewis*

The Faun's Bookshelf

The Faun's Bookshelf

C. S. Lewis on Why Myth Matters

Charlie W. Starr

BLACK SQUIRREL BOOKS® 🐿️°   Kent, Ohio

BLACK SQUIRREL BOOKS® 🐿®
Frisky, industrious black squirrels are a familiar sight on the Kent State
University campus and the inspiration for Black Squirrel Books®, a
trade imprint of The Kent State University Press.
www.KentStateUniversityPress.com

ISBN 978-1-60635-349-3
Manufactured in the United States of America

Cataloging information for this title is available at the Library of Congress.

22 21 20 19 18   5 4 3 2 1

Dedicated with love and thanks

to Ron and Doris Rife

Contents

Foreword

Devin Brown

Early in this fine book, Charlie Starr rightly highlights C. S. Lewis's belief that myth matters whether we realize it or not. And if someone had asked Lewis for a succinct answer to the question of *why* myth matters, he might have replied that myth matters because it reminds us that we and the world we live in are mythic. Today, as the voice of economic exigency whispers to us that the earth is ours to do with as we please and as the conception of what it means to be human gets smaller and smaller, these reminders are desperately needed.

One of Lewis's most significant encounters with myth—one of the times that it mattered most in his life—came on a frosty afternoon in March 1916 at the Leatherhead Train Station in the rural countryside southwest of London. Lewis was seventeen, and, in his routine of regular afternoon rambles, he had walked the three miles or so from the village of Great Bookham, where he was living at the time, and was waiting for the train to take him back. Standing on the platform in the fading light, he picked a worn book from the station's used-book stall. He had seen it before on previous walks to Leatherhead, but had always put it back. This time he decided to buy it.

The book was *Phantastes* by George MacDonald; later Lewis would compare his encounter with the myth he found between its covers to the first glimpse Dante had of Beatrice, an event so pivotal that Lewis would look back and, using Dante's phrase, declare, "Here begins the new life."

George Sayer, who was Lewis's pupil and friend as well as his biographer, writes at length about the impact *Phantastes* had on Lewis and concludes that MacDonald transformed Lewis's attitude toward the ordinary, material things around him, instilling them with their own spiritual quality. After this seminal encounter with myth, try as he might, Lewis could never again fully believe that the world could be reduced to just atoms and molecules.

One of the books from Mr. Tumnus's bookshelf is titled *Is Man a Myth?* If myth reminds us that our world is more than merely the matter it is made of, it also raises and answers the question "Is man mythic?"

Is man mythic? Are our decisions and the actions we take like those of the heroes we read about in the great stories of the past? Or are they more like the dull, inconsequential actions of J. Alfred Prufrock, T. S. Eliot's angst-ridden protagonist, who measures out his trivial, insignificant life with coffee spoons, a character whose biggest concerns each morning are where to part his hair and whether to wear his trousers rolled up.

Is man mythic? Do our lives have any individual meaning and purpose beyond what we choose to give them? Or are they, as Macbeth claims, just a tale told by an idiot where any significance they might seem to have is really just sound and fury, signifying nothing?

Is man mythic? Are our lives part of something greater? Or are we alone in the darkness, like a brief and feeble candle that in the end simply goes out?

Is man mythic? In *The Silver Chair*, Lewis's fourth installment in the Chronicles of Narnia, we find his most direct attempt to address this question head-on. In the book, Eustace and Jill must make a long and difficult journey in search of a missing prince. In chapter 10, they finally reach the Underland and are taken as captives inside the Dark Castle. Though they do not know it at the time, they have finally reached the object of their quest, the lost Prince Rilian.

The reason they don't realize whom they have found is because Rilian, somewhat like modern man, is under a spell, and this spell has caused him to forget who he is and where he belongs.

Eustace explains to the spellbound prince that they had been told to look for a message on the stones of the City Ruinous and that, while escaping from hostile giants, they had found the words UNDER ME. Rilian laughs and tells them that the words were in fact part of a longer message that was written not to them, but as the epitaph on the tomb of an ancient king. Jill and Eustace are devastated, for it seems that they have been taken in by a mere accident.

Like most young heroes on a quest, Jill and Eustace have been provided with an older, wiser companion, in this case an indomitable marsh-wiggle named Puddleglum, who urges them to reject Rilian's assertion and tells them that there are no accidents.

To Puddleglum's claim that there are no accidents, materialism would claim the opposite: there are *only* accidents. Any sense we might have of a presence of something or someone greater in our lives, any belief that we have been guided or directed by something beyond ourselves is all just make-believe, a nursery tale that might be useful to comfort frightened children, but one that should be discarded by serious adults. There are only accidents we are told again and again. In fact, life itself is just an accident—just the random, chance interaction of random, chance atoms and molecules.

Our heroes manage to free Rilian from the Silver Chair and the enchantment he is under. But then the Green Witch shows up. Realizing what has happened, she throws mind-numbing incense on the fire and begins to strum softly on her magic lute in an attempt to put all of them under her spell.

"There is no world but this one," she chants in a seductively sweet tone, giving voice to the central tenant of modern-day materialism.

The Silver Chair was published in 1953. If we jump ahead to 1957, we find that with the release of *The Last Battle* a year earlier, a groundswell of favorable opinion about the Narnia books was beginning to build. Meanwhile, in France, another celebrated author had just published a short story titled "The Guest," which in its own circle would become as famous as any work of Lewis's. Along with a series of works that included *The Stranger*, "The Guest" would help earn its author, Albert Camus, the Nobel Prize in Literature.

"The Guest" centers around a difficult decision thrust upon a French schoolmaster named Daru, who is stationed in Algeria. Daru's dilemma is whether or not to deliver to the French authorities an Arab who has committed murder. With no objective right or wrong, he has no guidelines to base his decision on. He will not be rewarded or recognized for making the right choice, for there is no right choice. Any decision Daru makes will have no moral significance beyond his own personal values.

In the end, Daru simply releases the Arab, instructing him to find shelter among his own people. But Daru's action proves pointless. Rather than accepting his freedom, the man takes the road to prison. The story ends with a stark statement of each individual's isolation in an empty, meaningless universe.

If Daru comes to see that he is alone and insignificant, Jill and Eustace learn the exact opposite. While Daru finds himself isolated and alienated in a world that is spiritually vacant, the protagonists in *The Silver Chair* find that they live in a world charged with a providential presence and come to see that they are connected in ways they never imagined.

In "The Guest," Camus shows us life that has no meaning other than what we choose to give it. In *The Silver Chair*, Lewis shows us that life is mythic.

Once the Green Witch is destroyed, our heroes still find themselves in a mess—the sea is rising, the lights are starting to go out, and they are surrounded by scary-looking Earthmen. But despite the hardships that await, Rilian urges them to all shake hands and then to descend into the city and, as he puts it, to take the adventure that is sent them.

Is life an adventure or just a series of unrelated accidents? Is man mythic or just the product of space plus time plus chance? Lewis's answers to these questions stand in stark contrast to what Camus would have us believe.

In a delightful scene from the film version of *The Lion, the Witch and the Wardrobe,* Mr. Beaver reveals an ancient prophecy that he claims the four children are helping to fulfill, and Peter replies, "I think you've made a mistake. We're not heroes."

And then to reinforce her brother's point, Susan explains, "We're from Finchley!"

Though the four children may have come from Finchley, that is not where their story ends. In the end, Peter Pevensie becomes King Peter the Magnificent, Susan the grouser becomes Queen Susan the Gentle, Edmund the former traitor becomes King Edmund the Just, and Lucy becomes Queen Lucy the Valiant. The Pevensie children both remain who they were, but also become something far greater—and, Lewis suggests, so shall we. There is a nobility to each of us, however ordinary we may seem.

Are our lives mythic? Through his own use of myth, Lewis reminds us again and again that they are meant to be. Charlie Starr makes a valuable contribution by helping us to more fully understand Lewis's position.

Acknowledgments

A good book is a collaboration, and I had a lot of collaborators. Several friends and colleagues committed to helping with content, editing, prayer, financial support, and more. In whichever of these ways they participated, my sincerest thanks go out to Arend Smilde, Stephen Thorson, Norbert Feinendegen, Michael Ward, Andrew Lazo, Jonathan Himes, Laura Schmidt, Charles A. Huttar, Devin Brown, Crystal Hurd, Don W. King, Diana Glyer, John M. Kirton II, Jennifer Neyhart, David Armstrong, Gary Newland, Bryan Rife, and Perry Stepp. Special thanks to Howard and Pat Falgout at OHT, and to Will Underwood at Kent State for believing in this book, and to the C. S. Lewis Company for their generosity in supplying permission to quote from Lewis's works.

Introduction

When most people visit a friend's house for the first time, they notice the decor, the furniture, the wallpaper, and the family photos. I make a beeline for the bookshelves. I want to see what they read—what they're interested in. I'll bet C. S. Lewis acted the same way, and the evidence I offer is the passage in *The Lion, the Witch and the Wardrobe* where little Lucy Pevensie has tea with her new friend, a faun named Mr. Tumnus. In the book, Lucy passes through a wardrobe in an old English manor into a completely different world. From summer in the English countryside, she enters a snowy winter landscape in a wood in the middle of which stands a lamppost. Almost immediately, a mythological creature who is half man, half goat (who isn't a myth at all in his own universe), carrying an umbrella and some parcels, comes upon Lucy. After a brief moment of mutual fright, the two get acquainted, and Mr. Tumnus the faun invites Lucy back to his home for tea. Lucy enters Tumnus's cozy cave and looks about the room as he prepares their refreshments. Along a wall, she surveys a shelf filled with books, from which we are given four representative titles:

1. *The Life and Letters of Silenus*
2. *Nymphs and Their Ways*

3. *Men, Monks, and Gamekeepers; a Study in Popular Legend*
4. *Is Man a Myth?*[1]

We learn nothing else of these or any other books in Mr. Tumnus's library.

But if we cannot see the books, it might still be possible for us to learn something from their titles—even though, in one sense, they don't exist. The works on this little faun's bookshelf are fictional, not in that they are fiction books, but in that, within Lewis's novel, he made up a set of books which don't exist *except* for their titles. Maybe there is too much to be made from too little information, but consider for a moment the fact that Lewis's good friend and fellow writer J. R. R. Tolkien once expressed his dislike for the whole of *The Lion, the Witch and the Wardrobe* by making fun of Tumnus's books. As he wrote to one of their mutual friends: "It really won't do, you know! I mean to say: '*Nymphs and Their Ways, The Love-Life of a Faun.*'"[2] Now I gather that if Tolkien (who got the second title wrong) can judge a book by its fictional cover, maybe we can learn something by focusing on the titles on Tumnus's bookshelf. Specifically, I think Lewis has a lot to teach us through the faun's little collection of books on the subject of myth, something Lewis cared about deeply and a topic that has fascinated Lewis scholars and fans for decades.

But does myth really matter? In an age of scientific fact and technological advancement, of culture wars and battles over what is right and just and who gets to say so, do we really need myths and mythological theories mucking up our understanding of truth and knowledge? I'll answer yes just by saying that some questions *have* to be answered. I've seen an illustration of this idea in the story of a man set before a firing squad under a sentence of execution. The man says his last words, the firing squad takes aim, the captain screams, "Fire!" and the riflemen shoot—but the man to be executed doesn't die. In fact, he remains standing there without a scratch. A situation like this is shouting for us to ask, "Why isn't this man dead?" There are many possible answers: the marksmen were bad shots (all of them?), the bullets were duds (same), the man to be executed is Superman, etc. But the point is that certain situations provoke questions that must be answered.

As a lover of literature and film, I have myself been interested in seeing two such questions answered. The first is a literary question: How is it possible that, in the twentieth century—an age of realistic, modernist fiction, an age of science and fact and apparent progress out of mythological, primitive, superstitious thinking—how is it possible that the mass of readers in that time (if not the literary critics) considered Tolkien's *The Lord of the Rings* to be the most important book of the century,[3] a book written at least in part with the very specific goal of producing a mythic tale for a mythless cultural age? The second is a film question, and it echoes the first, but with regard to George Lucas's *Star Wars* epic. The first film (and the franchise it spawned) is arguably the most influential movie (for good or ill) of the twentieth century. In an era of science and technology, George Lucas gave us some incredibly inaccurate science, based more on classic Hollywood film tropes from Hollywood's golden age than on scientific fact, and a plot narrative written according to a pattern he derived from Joseph Campbell's famous myth study, *The Hero with a Thousand Faces*.[4] During a decade (the 1970s) when G-rated films were passé (nearly killing Disney), sophisticated cynicism was the rage (it was the Woody Allen decade), heroes were gangsters (like Don Corleone in *The Godfather*), and the only stories of the supernatural were horror based (e.g., *The Exorcist*), *Star Wars* became an unlikely super success because it fed a need for which modern culture was starving.

Both Tolkien and Lucas purposely intended to write myths for an era in which myth was constantly being discredited as *mere* mythology: false stories invented by primitive (that is, "dumb") people to explain the world to their superstitious minds. The writer and the filmmaker succeeded in rejecting this attack on myth, and their texts potentially represent the most influential art pieces of the century, at least in terms of mass numbers. Understand what I am saying: the most important stories written in the modern age of scientific fact were myths and were purposely written to be mythic and give myths to an age that the authors thought desperately needed it.

Since then, the impact of mythic tales on our culture has only increased—to the point, for example, that what used to be the stuff of comic book stories (mostly for young readers and then mostly for boys) has developed into a mass industry of blockbuster superhero movies. From the occasional *Batman* or *X-Men* movie, we have moved into a period of five or six superhero blockbusters per year plus several television spin-off series. We have invented our gods, put them in spandex, and given them stories—tales that draw us to dark temples (now called movie theaters) where we offer monetary sacrifices to the gatekeepers (usually young acolytes off for the summer from school), make our votive offerings to obtain sacrificial corn (of the popping variety), and watch in darkness and firelight as the digital bards spin their tales (Plato might cringe at our voluntary return to his allegorical cave).

This then is my point: Myth matters to us, whether we realize it or not. It has a powerful effect on us, whether we're willing to admit it or not. And this *mattering* and this *powerful affecting* demand that we ask why. These are questions C. S. Lewis can help us answer. Lewis was himself no slouch when it came to writing mythic tales. In his Space Trilogy—*Out of the Silent Planet, Perelandra,* and *That Hideous Strength*—he created science fiction tales that explored and brought myth to life, long before George Lucas would take us to a galaxy far, far away. In *The Great Divorce,* Lewis explored heaven and its theological implications through mythic landscapes, and his favorite novel (what many critics think to be his greatest), *Till We Have Faces,* fused myth with modern psychological characterization to create encounters with the divine for modern culture. Then, of course, there are the Chronicles of Narnia, a series of seven children's books that have sold over 100 million copies in sixty years. The series could be described in many ways, but one of these, as we see in Mr. Tumnus's library, is as a series of mythic stories and explorations of myth. Myth *matters,* and the faun's bookshelf gives us a starting point for accessing what C. S. Lewis can teach us about it. And myth is a *mystery,* one that Tumnus's books can help us solve.

Part I
Folios and Fauns

CHAPTER ONE

Of the Making of Many (Fake) Books

Lewis and Mythopoeia

Fictitious Books of Fiction

The four nonexistent books in Tumnus's library aren't the only ones Lewis made up. He was fond of inventing imaginary book titles, book passages, and even authors. Doing so was part of a myth-oriented theory of writing Lewis shared with Tolkien, which we'll consider after a look at Lewis's fictional fictions.

Lewis once described himself as the product of "endless books."[1] His father collected books and kept them all—they filled Lewis's childhood home, and he was allowed to read whichever books he liked. As a result of this early enchantment with books, Lewis himself wrote almost four dozen books in his lifetime (with much more of his written material collected after his death) and even made up books he didn't write.

Of these, first of all, there are books to which Lewis gave a title or an author or both, but that have no content. These include another Narnian book entitled *Grammatical Garden or the Arbour of Accidence Pleasantlie Open'd to Tender Wits* by Pulverulentus Siccus, one of the textbooks used by Dr. Cornelius to teach the young Prince Caspian.[2] The Latin of the author's name is an invention and a joke. *Pulver* means "dust," *lentus* means "slow," and *siccus* means "dry." For Caspian, who prefers to learn about

Narnian history, the study of grammar is all of these things.[3] Another book in this category, also of the literary teacher's variety, is written by Lewis's fictional philologist hero, Dr. Elwin Ransom; it's called *Dialect and Semantics*[4] and represents Ransom's work as a university philologist.[5]

While on Mars, Ransom also gives thought to writing a book or two on the language he later learns is called "Old Solar" (properly called "Hlab-Eribol-ef-Cordi," or the "Speech of the Field of Arbol").[6] Ransom considers such titles as *An Introduction to the Malacandrian Language, The Lunar Verb,* and *A Concise Martian-English Dictionary.*[7] That the fictional Ransom might have fictionally written these books is a real fictional possibility. Though the fictional Lewis narrator (the Lewis who appears at the end of *Out of the Silent Planet* and at the beginning of *Perelandra*) claims Ransom did not write any books on the Martian language,[8] Ransom might have needed them when he translated *The Screwtape Letters.*

My tongue-in-cheek reference here is to Lewis's original introduction for *The Screwtape Letters.* While half or so of that text appears at the beginning of the book, several sentences were cut from final publication.[9] In the *missing* text, Lewis, as fictional author, claims that he got Screwtape's letters from Ransom, who had learned how to read the Old Solar language, which all creatures speak outside the realm of Earth. In the end, whether the decision was made by Lewis or his publisher, these imaginary connections with *Silent Planet* were removed from *The Screwtape Letters.* Still, they give us the opportunity to speculate that Ransom *did* write his Malacandrian grammar and made translating the demonic letters possible. A point not to be overlooked here is that Lewis didn't just make up book titles, he also fictionalized himself and our world. He is a character in two of the Ransom books, in the published *Screwtape* introduction (where he pretends to have obtained the letters, but won't say how nor why he can read them), and in *The Great Divorce.*

In the Space Trilogy, especially, Lewis is then able to reverse realities: At the end of *Out of the Silent Planet*, he talks as if the events of the book really happened by making himself a character in the story. In chapter 22, Lewis-the-narrator begins to write as if the story were real. He says it's time to take off the mask and inform the reader of the real reason the book was written.[10] Then he tells the reader that *Ransom* is a pseudonym (given to protect the *real* Ransom's identity) and that Ransom has himself chosen not to tell of his marvelous adventures. Lewis-the-narrator claims that this is the point he enters the story.[11] He says he knows Dr. Ransom professionally, having consulted with him about literature and philology.[12] He then writes of how he first learned of Ransom's story: After finding an obscure reference in a medieval text from the twelfth century by a writer named Bernardus Silvestris (who actually existed and is *not* a fictional author), a peculiar word piqued the Lewis-narrator's interest. In describing a journey through the heavens, Silvestris uses the word *Oyerses*[13] (which are the arch-angelic Oyarsas, or Oyéresu, appearing in all three books of the Space Trilogy); the fictional Lewis writes to consult with Ransom on any insights he might have into this obscure word. The result is that Ransom invites him to visit for a weekend, during which he tells Lewis the entire story. Lewis continues the ruse, even giving a reason for the work to *appear* to be fictional,[14] and ends the book with a postscript of extracts out of letters written to Lewis by the real Ransom.[15] Lewis was so convincing that at least one fan of *Silent Planet* actually wrote him, asking him to clarify whether the book was fact or fiction.[16]

Another medieval author to appear in the Ransom books is Natvilcius, but, while Silvestrus was real, this individual is completely made up.[17] In a footnote for chapter 1 of *Perelandra*, Lewis references Natvilcius's *De Aethereo et aerio Corpore, Basel*, a nonexistent book.[18] The joke being played, though, is that the name *Natvilcius* is a Latin version of a favorite Lewis pseudonym, the

Old English *Nat Whilk*, which means "I know not whom." Lewis often used *Nat Whilk* and *N. W.* as pseudonyms when he published poems;[19] likewise, when he felt that his book *A Grief Observed* might be too controversial, he asked that it be published under the name *N. W. Clerk*, which essentially translates as "an unknown writer."

In his essay, "Fern-seed and Elephants," Lewis sarcastically critiques one author's work by using an invented book title. In this talk on the trend in biblical criticism to demythologize the Bible, Lewis questions a number of contemporary theologians, not for being bad biblical scholars, but for being bad literary critics—doubting their ability, for example, to recognize a myth or fable when they see one. In one instance, he questions the famous New Testament scholar Rudolf Bultmann for saying that the personality of Christ does not appear in the Gospels.[20] After offering counterpoints to this claim, Lewis writes that he is beginning to think that Bultmann's idea of personality is something Lewis would refer to as quite impersonal, the kind of description we'd get from an obituary, an article out of Oxford's *Dictionary of National Biography*, or a "Victorian *Life and Letters of Yeshua-Bar Yosef* in three volumes with photographs."[21]

Other made-up books get brief reference without titles throughout Lewis's fiction. In *The Voyage of the Dawn Treader*, we read of Eustace and his love for books of facts and figures, filled with farming structures and plump foreign children exercising in modern educational facilities.[22] These get referred to as the wrong kinds of books,[23] but Eustace's nemesis and eventual friend, Reepicheep, appears to have a good library back in Narnia.[24] Also in *Dawn Treader*, Lucy reads through the magician's book (in his vast library filled from floor to ceiling with books[25]), discovering all manner of wonderful and dangerous spells and stories.[26]

In *The Silver Chair*, the giants have a cookbook with recipes for cooking both humans and marsh-wiggles.[27] The Calormenes of

The Horse and His Boy write proverbs,[28] the hrossa of *Silent Planet* make poetry,[29] and the sorns in the same novel have books in the form of scrolls[30]—though not many because, as the wise sorn Augray notes, it's better to remember than to write down. *That Hideous Strength* refers to a book written by an ancestor of Jane's regarding a famous historical battle at Worcester.[31] This imaginary book was supposedly written by a man who wasn't at the battle, but had dreamed the events with complete accuracy and recorded them. Additionally, the Episcopal ghost in *The Great Divorce* wrote several books of liberal theology that earned him fame in certain circles.[32]

The library of Glome in *Till We Have Faces* contains classical books that actually existed (some of which have been lost to history—we only know them by name today).[33] We could even add *Till We Have Faces* itself as an imaginary work in the sense that we get from it another narrator who claims that it is based on real events. At the beginning of the novel, the main character, Orual, tells us that she is writing this book as an argument against the gods. In her world, the book is historical, autobiographical, not a work of fiction. Lewis also fictionalizes an actual classical work in the form of his essay, "Xmas and Christmas," which he claims to be a lost chapter from the *Histories* of Herodotus.[34]

Then there is the story of Ezekiel Bulver.[35] He is the imaginary inventor of Bulverism, a technique for argument that Lewis found common in the twentieth century. In this technique, an opponent doesn't argue that a person's *ideas* are wrong, but argues that the *person* is wrong (like when someone calls you a *bigot* for having a politically incorrect moral stance). The fictional Bulver first notices this when he is only five years old: his parents are arguing a problem in math, and his mother claims her husband believes what he does only because he is a man.[36] Bulver immediately realizes that you don't have to refute an argument, just attack the person for whatever is the cause of his narrow-mindedness. Bulver then (fictionally speaking) becomes one of the great movers of the century; Lewis plans on eventually writing the biography of this imaginary man.

Besides fictional books and authors and pseudonyms, there is also an instance of Lewis's renaming an *actual* book used in English education—a book that Lewis critiqued heavily in *The Abolition of Man*. Because he made such an extended attack on this book and its authors, he gave them anonymous names: for the book, *The Green Book,* and for the authors, Titius and Gaius.[37] Lewis also gives a pseudonym to (or else completely invents) his friend Corineus, with whom he has a disagreement in the essay "Myth Became Fact."[38]

Next, there are Lewis's fake letters. *The Screwtape Letters* are, of course, an invention, but so are the *Letters to Malcolm*. Malcolm wasn't a real person; Lewis used the method of writing letters to a fictional friend in order to talk about prayer—his attempts to deal with prayer in more formal or philosophical ways (as with *The Problem of Pain* or *Miracles*) had ended with incomplete manuscripts.[39]

Finally, we get Lewis's fake commentaries. As a professor of medieval and Renaissance literature, Lewis wrote numerous actual works of literary criticism, including *The Allegory of Love; A Preface to Paradise Lost;* and *English Literature in the Sixteenth Century, Excluding Drama*. He also wrote a few fake critical works. When Adam Fox was up for a poetry chair at Oxford University, Lewis wrote an anonymous critique of Fox's work as if it had been one of Johnson's *Lives of the English Poets,* which Johnson began in 1740. Lewis called it "From Johnson's *Life of Fox*."[40] Then there is an unpublished postscript that Lewis sent to his friend Owen Barfield at the end of a letter dated March 22, 1932. The postscript—which is wonderfully obscure—imagines a commentary originating in the future. An unnamed author is studying the letters of Lewis and Barfield and commenting on notes and events that fictionally happened decades (or perhaps longer) ago. This future Lewis scholar references specific lines in Lewis's letter, and includes arguments against or agreements with other (nonexistent) Lewis/Barfield scholars; the text even cites a letter Barfield wrote in 1950 (remember, this fake commentary was actually written by Lewis in 1932) in which Barfield claims that everything he learned about language he learned from C. S. Lewis,[41] a hilarious statement for those who know the truth of the matter, which is that Barfield's work on the history of language had a huge impact on Lewis's thinking.

But the most famous fictional critical work by Lewis is one he wrote for Tolkien, probably in 1930. For a very long time, very few people read anything of Tolkien's Middle-earth fiction because he hadn't published it. But Lewis was an early fan of the stories that would eventually make their way in one form or another into the *Silmarillion* and Christopher Tolkien's twelve-volume *History of Middle-earth.* In 1929, Tolkien gave Lewis the manuscript of his *Lay of Leithian* to read and critique. The lay is a poetic telling of Tolkien's tale of Beren and Luthien from the First Age of Middle-earth. Instead of merely sending Tolkien notes on the text, Lewis wrote his critique as if he were a specialist in this ancient history, writing about a real document. In the way that a scholar of medieval literature would discuss lines from Beowulf or various versions of the King Arthur tales—their language and the history of their textual transmission—Lewis commented on Tolkien's *Lay of Leithian* as if it had been written thousands of years ago about long-existing legends.[42] So in the same way that he made *Out of the Silent Planet* seem to be an actual event, so did Lewis make Tolkien's Middle-earth out to be a real place in ancient history, with an even longer history of textual transmission (the history of how the version we have of the *Lay* today came to us over the centuries). Tolkien did the same thing himself. In *The Lord of the Rings,* Tolkien claims the book to be not an invention, but a translation from an ancient book called the *Red Book of Westmarch.*[43] Here we can add one final example: in *That Hideous Strength,* Lewis makes Tolkien's fictional Númenor (from the Second Age of Middle-earth—chronicled in the *Silmarillion*) a part of Ransom's fictional world, treating it as if it too really existed.[44]

In part, Lewis and Tolkien are playing a joke on us, but their choice to connect their various works of fiction to reality also represents something they both believed about the nature of fiction writing—especially the writing of fantasy tales. And here we begin our first foray into the study of myth: the theory of mythopoeia, which Tolkien and Lewis shared.[45]

Mythopoeia

The famous twentieth-century literary critic Northrop Frye complimented C. S. Lewis by including him in a group of writers about whom he said, "many learned and recondite writers whose work requires patient study are explicitly mythopoeic writers."[46] Lewis himself offers a hint at defining the theory of mythopoeia in his review of *The Hobbit*, which he describes as belonging to a certain small group of books that have one thing in common: each one contains a complete world, one that seems to have been in existence long before the stories we encounter there take place.[47] In "On Science-Fiction," Lewis identifies a type of sci-fi story that he calls mythopoeic. These are characterized by strange settings—entire worlds—that don't need to be probable in any scientific way; they just need to be wondrous, beautiful, or vaguely suggestive.[48] In the same essay Lewis labels fairy tales and fantasies as mythopoeic.[49]

Lewis gets even more specific in his review of *The Fellowship of the Ring*. There he writes that Tolkien's great myth at moments achieves a level of invention where the author has produced something that isn't even his own—that reads as if it comes to the author by intuitive revelation, not artistic invention;[50] Tolkien's world is a world unto itself. To describe this kind of writing, Lewis uses the terms *mythopoeia* and *sub-creation* (a term that Tolkien invented and both he and Lewis used). Lewis describes mythopoeia as a human function intended not to comment on life, but to allow an author to create an entire world of his own.[51] Lewis labels *The Fellowship of the Ring* the most thorough example of sub-creation in literature,[52] claiming that the novel possesses the quality of cosmos-making that defines mythopoeia and sub-creation: beyond the story alone, Tolkien creates the "whole world in which it is to move, with its own theology, myths, geography, history, palaeography, languages, and orders of beings."[53]

Tolkien's own explanation of sub-creation is laid out in his lengthy essay "On Fairy-Stories." He relates the idea to myth and says that the story-maker who is capable of creating literary belief in a reader proves himself successful at sub-creation. He creates a "Secondary World" that readers can enter; in that world, what he tells us is true for that world and accords with the rules of that creation.[54] This sub-created world will have an "inner consistency of reality" that inspires "Secondary Belief"[55]—that is, the sub-created world will be one that the reader can imaginatively enter and accept as a reality of its own.

Tolkien explains the theological importance of mythopoeic sub-creation in his poem "Mythopoeia." The poem was occasioned by a conversation between Tolkien and Lewis (ultimately leading to Lewis's return to Christianity) in which Lewis (at that time) argued that myth had no truth-value. Tolkien said that it did: Just as words are inventions about objects—we use the word *tree* to denote a tall, barked flora with many branches and green leaves—so myths are inventions about reality; since they are about reality, they have truth-value. In the subsequent poem, Tolkien goes so far as to suggest that reality has no meaning to us until we assign it *mythic* meaning. He says, for example, that no one can see the stars who doesn't see them initially as "of living silver made that sudden burst / to flame like flowers beneath an ancient song. . . ."[56]

Tolkien further suggests that, in making myth, we conform to a divine mandate, mimicking the creative activity of God. Though we may be fallen, and sometimes wrongly invent false gods out of the world, we're still called to this activity of myth-making (perhaps in the same way God called Adam to name the animals in Genesis). Essentially, Tolkien believed that, since we are created in God's image and God is a creator, we follow in God's footsteps by acting as sub-creators. We are not meant to worship the world, but to make worlds of our own out of our experiences of it. And when we create worlds in our imaginations as completely as possible—whole histories behind the stories we are telling, with whole peoples, cultures, languages, and geographies—we are imitating God, which delights both Him and us. Mythopoeic literature, then, is literature that operates within an entire cosmos, a cosmos that is often entirely invented. [57]

What then is the connection between mythopoeia and Lewis's imaginary books? Some may say that Tolkien more than Lewis represents a mythopoeic ideal. However, the truth is that both writers believed in creating mythic worlds that were as imaginatively complete as possible. This is apparent in the fact that they both created books that don't exist. Lewis tells us that the great mythopoeic quality of Tolkien's *The Lord of the Rings* is that, when we read it, we feel we are entering a world that has already been going on for a very long time. With a light, subtle touch, Lewis achieves the same quality by giving us some of the titles on Mr. Tumnus's bookshelf. We don't know the content of the books, but the titles hint at a larger world. We go exploring those titles on the off chance that they may show us something of what's been going on in that world for ages past.

CHAPTER TWO

Fauns and Their Fantasies

 Before we dive into the books on his shelf, we should learn something of Mr. Tumnus and other fauns like him. After all, Tumnus was the impetus for the entire Narniad! Without this little faun, we might have never had *The Chronicles of Narnia*. Lewis notes many times that these books began with pictures in his head. Regarding *The Lion, the Witch and the Wardrobe* specifically, he wrote that it started with the "picture of a Faun carrying an umbrella and parcels in a snowy wood," a picture which had been in Lewis's head since he was sixteen. Besides this, the more we understand fauns in general, the more we'll understand their books.[1]

There is some speculation about the origin of Tumnus's name. It sounds Latin and may refer either to a hill (because Tumnus lives under a hill) or a shape-shifting forest god.[2] Neither of these possibilities inspires us to explore any deeper meanings, but there are several fauns in *Prince Caspian* whose names are worth a brief look. These fauns dance around a fire with the young prince and are named much after the fashion of Tolkien's dwarves in *The Hobbit*. Like Tumnus, they have Latin-sounding names, such as Mentius, Obentinus, Dumnus, and Nimienus.[3] While these names may serve merely to connect the fauns to their Roman roots in classical mythology, Paul Ford has offered for Dumnus a connection to the Latin word *dumus,*

a "thicket, thornbush [or] bramble in which fauns might be expected to live,"[4] and for *Mentius* he points to the Latin *mentior,* which refers to a liar or a cheat—something fauns might be prone to do (at least in the classic myths).[5]

Lewis describes what fauns look like when Lucy and Tumnus first meet. Tumnus isn't much taller than Lucy, who is only eight years old. From the waist up he looks like a man, but his legs are goat-shaped with hooves. He also has a tail that he carries over his arm to keep it out of the snow. His skin is reddish, his hair is curly, his beard short and pointed, and he has a pair of horns.[6] Lewis adds in *Prince Caspian* that fauns are bare chested, and their unusual faces seem at once both merry and mournful.[7]

Fauns are frequently lumped into a group with satyrs, nymphs, dryads, and naiads, often under the name *sylvan*—a word signifying woods, forests, or anything associated with the forest (the term may also designate yet another separate mythical species). Of whatever sort, sylvans as a group are essentially nature creatures—belonging to the wild world of forests and streams (though not oceans). Sometimes they are animals; sometimes they are spirits of water and trees. Dryads and naiads are kinds of nymphs—with dryads being tree spirits and naiads being water spirits—though the terms can be used interchangeably.

While fauns and satyrs are both half man, they are sometimes separate creatures and sometimes the same. In classical mythology, they are occasionally differentiated by fauns being half goat and satyrs being half horse, but this distinction is fluid depending on the era in history.[8] Things become even more convoluted in Roman mythology with the gods Faunus, Sylvanus, and Pan. Fauns become attached especially to both Faunus and Pan, becoming the sons and followers of Pan in some tales. So we have to look a little at *these* mythic beings as well.

Lewis's last novel, *Till We Have Faces,* provides an interesting sidenote regarding the blended yet distinct identities of these various creatures. In that book, the gods flow in and out of each other. As the old priest explains, the local goddess, Ungit (Aphrodite), and her son, the Shadowbrute (Cupid), have a mysterious relationship in which each may be the other as well—sometimes separate, sometimes the same at once.[9] This is possible because "the gods flow in and out of one another like eddies on a river, and nothing that is said clearly can be said truly about them."[10] I have often thought that Lewis was suggesting in this theme something of the divine, "super-personal" life of God that he talks about in *Mere Christianity*—an echo of God's Trinitarian nature.

Take, for example, Lewis's description of the Trinitarian life as it flows in and out of us as well as God in prayer: When a Christian kneels to pray, he is trying to communicate with God, but he also knows that what is motivating him to pray is the Spirit of God living inside him and that he is being helped to pray by Christ who is working beside him, both helping and praying for the Christian as he prays.[11] In this example God is simultaneously the one whom the man is praying to, the power inside the man urging him to pray, and the bridge that makes it possible for his prayers to reach God. Lewis sees the whole activity of the three-personed God going on in this moment of prayer; in this encounter the man is being pulled up into the same kind of super-personal life in which God participates: the man is "being pulled into God, by God, while still remaining himself."[12] Lewis believes that humanity's ultimate goal is to enter into a spiritual life that reflects the super-personal nature of God—one in which we remain ourselves, while yet becoming more than ourselves; one in which we share in a many-in-one life, becoming types of the head for which we, in the church, become the body. He believes that all Christians are meant to become little Christs and that this is the very reason we become Christians.[13]

But let's return to the connections between fauns and the other sylvan creatures. These explain something of the first two book titles from Tumnus's library: *The Life and Letters of Silenus* and *Nymphs and Their Ways.* Fauns enjoyed spending time with nymphs and with Bacchus and his old sidekick, Silenus. But in the White Witch's hundred years of winter, the naiads were doubtless frozen in the rivers and streams, the dryads did no dancing, and Silenus was not to be seen; so during this time the best Tumnus could do was read about them and hope to see them someday—just as we might hope, when we read about elves in the Greenwood, hobbits in the Shire, talking animals in Narnia, and the great lion Aslan.

Most of what Lewis tells us about fauns and other sylvans he does through the lenses of medieval literature and thought. In *The Allegory of Love,* Lewis's study of medieval love poetry, he writes that "Between earth and moon dwell the 'airish' folk, and on the earth's surface those long-livers who are fairies undisguised, for all their classical names."[14] Then he quotes a medieval text, describing "Silvans, Pans, and Nerei," who dwell in earth's most wonderful places—grassy ridges, flowering mountaintops, bright streams, green woods—living long lives because their bodies are pure in element, though they do eventually die.[15] Lewis introduces these creatures more completely in *The Discarded Image,* his comprehensive overview of medieval thought and imagination. He refers to them as the *Longaevi,* the "long-livers" who dwell between earth and air and whose position in the grand Christian vision of the era is suspect. Lewis finds the term in a medieval writer named Martianus Capella, who refers to troops of "*Longaevi* who haunt woods, glades, and groves, and lakes and springs and brooks." Capella labels these creatures as "Pans, Fauns...Satyrs, Silvans, Nymphs."[16] Their reputation fluctuates throughout the Middle Ages, but these were among a long list of creatures adults would use to frighten their children.[17] And Lewis notes that St. Augustine once gave thought to how such "semi-human creatures" might fit into the Christian universe—although Augustine decided not to draw any conclusions until he knew whether such beings actually existed.[18]

As mentioned, fauns are tied closely to the god Faunus, to satyrs, and to Pan. The god Faunus was a woodland god who was credited for any sudden, unexplainable noises people heard in the forest. He was eventually combined with both Pan and Sylvanus.[19] Lewis tells us of a story about Faunus in Spenser's *Faerie Queene* in which the god tricks a nymph into helping him see the goddess Diana naked. He gets his wish, but in doing so fails to maintain a silent reverence—he laughs out loud,[20] suggesting that Faunus represents existence on a purely natural level, one beneath the pure divinity represented by the goddess.[21] We may see here something of why Tumnus struggles to do the right thing with regard to Lucy. Remember that his initial plan is to take what for him must also be a magical (though young) lady and betray her to the White Witch. But unlike Faunus, who is thwarted by his laughter and irreverence, Tumnus dissolves into tears and contrition and changes his plans, proving himself nobler than his Spenserian counterpart.

Lewis makes just a few and rather obscure references to Pan in his writings.[22] But sources on mythology tell us that Pan was connected to Silenus and Bacchus (the Roman name for Dionysus) and that he was, like a faun, part man and part goat; he is most famous for the invention of the Pan pipe made from marsh reeds. Not by coincidence, Mr. Tumnus plays a flute that appears to be made of straw, and the song he plays makes Lucy want to "cry and laugh and dance and go to sleep all at the same time."[23] Pan's mother was a nymph (so perhaps Tumnus's interest in nymphs is also familial), and he fell in love with numerous nymphs, most famously Syrinx, for whom his pipe is named.[24] So Pan was a womanizer (or nymph-anizer), but Lewis recasts the myth for his children's book into the form of a kindly little faun who must decide how best to treat his innocent female guest.

Tumnus is also a voice against the antics of Pan in *The Horse and His Boy* in his support of Susan's refusal to marry Rabadash of Tashbaan, especially as Rabadash intends to force the marriage.[25] Interestingly, Pan has a distant connection to Rabadash, who gets turned into a donkey at the end of the novel.[26] The connection is a story about Apollo and Midas. The myth goes that Pan and Apollo had a musical duel that everyone agreed the great god won—everyone except for Midas. Apollo was so angered by this stupidity that he condemned Midas to having the ears of a donkey.[27]

We've looked at the connection between satyrs[28] and fauns; I'll only add that satyrs are closely associated with Bacchus, the Roman god of agriculture, wine, and fertility; they love to dance and sing; they love to chase maenads through the woods.[29] Lewis tells us that, in Spenser, they represent nature in its pristine, unspoiled form.[30] This is worth mentioning in the context of the Narnian winter. The winter looks beautiful and magical to us, especially in the way it's portrayed in film versions of *The Lion, the Witch and the Wardrobe,* but the witch's winter is a deadly beauty, a corruption—or at least a literal freezing—of nature. Satyrs or fauns cannot dance in such woods.

And so, while we'll have more to say about the significance of fauns in Lewis's Narnia Chronicles, we can come to the preliminary conclusion that these creatures are symbolic of nature-in-celebration—of the kind of abundant life Jesus promised his disciples in the Gospels.[31] Lewis once described the encounter between Lucy and Tumnus as a "rather fine high tea given by a hospitable faun to the little girl who was my heroine."[32] That Tumnus was a hospitable faun was probably significant to Lewis not only by symbolic association, but by personal experience. Why choose food as a symbol of abundance and blessing? One reason may be that, after World War II, prosperity did not quickly return to England, and the rationing protocols of wartime were extended beyond the early days of victory. A well-known story from Lewis's life is of the time an American sent him a ham. This morsel was converted into a feast that

Lewis and his fellow Inklings[33] relished given the food limits they faced in 1948.[34] As a result, the most famous Inklings letter of all time was sent to the generous provider of the feast. It read, "The undersigned, having just partaken of your ham, have drunk your health," and was signed by both Lewis brothers, by Tolkien and his son Christopher, and by David Cecil, Colin Hardie, and others.[35] As a celebrant of nature and abundant life, Tumnus couldn't help but offer from his stores an amazing meal for Lucy. One imagines that the difficulty of obtaining such a feast amid the hundred-year Narnian winter must have been as hard as finding a ham in England in wartime. Tumnus the hospitable faun offered it anyway.

CHAPTER THREE

Might Myth Be Real?

Looking around Tumnus's house, Lucy notices a shelf filled with books, but we only get four representative titles, suggesting that the other books on the shelf are similar in content. In looking at these four books, though, we get immediate insight. The books can be divided into two categories: In the first category, our classical myths are made Narnian reality: *The Life and Letters of Silenus* and *Nymphs and Their Ways*. In the second category, we're given books in which *our* reality is made Narnian myth: *Men, Monks, and Gamekeepers* and *Is Man a Myth?* And here we encounter an idea that appears throughout Lewis's written thought, that our reality might be myth in some other world, and vice versa.

For example, in his story "Forms of Things Unknown," Lewis writes about an astronaut who lands on the moon in search of missing explorers who have gone before him. He discovers a statue of one of these astronauts, only to turn and realize too late that it was no statue—he himself is turned to stone by the gaze of Medusa.[1] And so what is myth on earth is reality in other worlds. We see this idea played out in reverse in Narnia when the Narnians are amazed to discover that our Earth isn't flat but round.[2]

In the first of his science-fiction novels, *Out of the Silent Planet*, Lewis's protagonist, Ransom, looks down upon the canals of Mars as he leaves the planet and ponders how such massive feats of engineering were possible. He wonders if perhaps the explanation he was given was only mythological, and he even considers the possibility that the "distinction between history and mythology might be itself meaningless outside the Earth."[3] This is a thought Ransom experiences several times on Venus in the book *Perelandra*. Early in the novel he sees a small, red dragon wrapped around a tree filled with golden fruit; immediately he thinks of the Garden of the Hesperides from Greek mythology—the magical garden where the fruit of the gods resides, a fruit that makes its eater immortal.[4] Its connections to Eden fit perfectly with the paradisal planet that Ransom has come to—a planet where Tor and Tinidril, another Eve and Adam, are about to face temptation just as their counterparts did on Earth. Later, Ransom wonders if he's been sent to that planet to enact a myth;[5] eventually he comes to realize that outside the fallen Earth, there might be no division between myth and fact.[6] At one point in the novel, upon considering the new myths surrounding evolution, Ransom even speculates that the myths of antiquity were more true than modern ones, and this makes him wonder if there actually had been times in history when satyrs danced in the woods of Italy.[7]

So, again, what appears as myth in our world may be a reality in some other. But what exactly does this mean—what point is Lewis trying to make? Is he only doing fiction, or is he speculating about things he believes genuinely possible? In his vision at the end of *Perelandra*, Ransom is shown that our human conception of the gods comes in part from real angelic powers bound to the other planets in our solar system. There are governing angels of Mars and Venus and the other planets. Ransom wonders how knowledge of such beings could come to the old poets of Earth. How did the pagan writers learn to associate Ares with war and Aphrodite with a birth from the foaming sea? The angelic beings Ransom encounters tell him that such knowledge comes indirectly and through multiple stages. He learns that there is an

> environment of minds as well as of space. The universe is one— a spider's web wherein each mind lives along every line, a vast whispering gallery. . . . Memory passes through the womb and hovers in the air. The Muse is . . . real . . . [and a] faint breath . . . reaches even the late generations. Our mythology is based on a solider reality than we dream: but it is also at an almost infinite distance from that base.[8]

Upon hearing this, Ransom understands what mythology really is: "gleams of celestial strength and beauty falling on a jungle of filth and imbecility."[9] Lewis wants us to see that there may be more of a connection between reality and myth than we have thought possible, and he wants us to see that myth can show us truth. A point Lewis makes throughout his writing (both fiction and nonfiction) is that myth has epistemological value—it provides us knowledge (in ways that other methods of communication cannot). He believes our minds are not completely autonomous; we are interconnected with other minds—not just in this world, but in spiritual realms above us. This idea is suggested in the negative by Lewis's conception of demonic influence as it is portrayed in *The Screwtape Letters*. There, Screwtape urges the demon Wormwood to tempt his patient through a careful management of his thought life.[10] In *Perelandra*, Lewis suggests the possibility that God influences our thoughts even when we don't know He's doing it—and He does this especially in our imaginations through myth.

Lewis argues this idea in the allegory of his own conversion, *The Pilgrim's Regress*. In book 8, chapter 8, the protagonist, John, meets an old hermit who is the embodiment of history. The hermit tells John that the Landlord (God) has attempted to communicate to the tenants (mankind) primarily in two ways: first, through a series of rules (representing natural law and the call of conscience initially, and then the code of ethics handed to us through the people of Israel); second, through a series of pictures (representing myth). The Enemy of the Landlord (Satan) convinced many of the tenants the Landlord didn't exist and kept watch to make sure no information about Him got through to them. John asks if this strategy was successful, and History replies that it was not. Though many people thought the Enemy fooled the tenants by making up fake stories about the Landlord, History claims that he has visited Pagus—the land of pagan beliefs and worship—often enough to know that the truth isn't that simple. History tells John that the Landlord was successful at getting many messages through the resistance. John asks him what kind of messages, and History answers that the messages were "mostly pictures."[11]

Lewis's idea is that God spoke to pagan peoples even through their pagan religions—through their myths and poets. Their gods may have been false, but pictures were still being sent to them by God—not as words of truth spoken propositionally through prophets, but as stories, symbols, and plot elements spoken imaginatively through poets and storytellers. In an early copy of The Pilgrim's Regress that Lewis himself annotated by hand, he wrote the following comment next to History's words about pictures: "There is, in my opinion, a divine element in most mythologies."[12] As Lewis explains in Mere Christianity, God sent to us "what I call good dreams: I mean those queer stories scattered all through the heathen religions about a god who dies and comes to life again and, by his death, has somehow given new life to men."[13] One of myth's connections to reality, then, is epistemological—that is, myth is capable of showing us something of the nature of reality. It can show us truth.[14]

But Lewis is making another point as well: he is saying that the reality we see around us is not all there is. He believes creation is hierarchical, even multidimensional. There are levels to reality, and Lewis both explains and offers mythic images of this idea throughout his writing. In his essay, "Miracles," he outright tells us that "there might be Natures piled upon Natures"[15] and that, at the least, there is nature as we know it and the supernature beyond.[16] In his science fiction, he gives us an image of multiple realities, with our myths being real on the moon and on other planets. In his fantasy the same image comes in two forms. The first of these is the depiction of parallel realities (rather than hierarchical ones). Narnia is a world next-door to ours—just through the wardrobe. But it's not a part of our universe—it's part of some other.[17] The same is true of the old, dying world of Charn in *The Magician's Nephew*. These and even many other natures are interconnected via the Wood Between the Worlds in which Digory and Polly discover an uncountable number of pools, each of which appears to lead to a whole new universe.[18]

In Lewis's fantasy, the second image of multiple realities is a hierarchical one—the idea of natures on top of natures. It is presented powerfully in *The Great Divorce* and *The Last Battle*. In *Divorce,* Heaven is so utterly real—so full of Being—that the souls who first arrive there are little more than ghostly "stains on the brightness of that air."[19] They are so lacking in reality or Being that they don't even bend the blades of grass beneath their feet. The narrator of the novel is told that hell is the size of a pebble on earth and smaller than an atom in heaven.[20]

In *The Last Battle,* when the heroes of Narnia come into Aslan's country, it seems familiar to them, though it is not any place they've been before. Soon they come to realize the truth: it is familiar to them because it's Narnia—only this is the *real* Narnia, bigger and better, the Narnia on which the old one was modeled, of which the old one was just a shadowy copy.[21] The narrator tries to explain how this new Narnia is the real one and as different as conscious life is from a dream,[22] but he has a difficult time doing so. He settles on an illustration: imagine being in a room with a window that looks out onto a beautiful landscape or sea-scape. Then imagine turning from the window and catching a glimpse of that same landscape or seascape in a mirror on an opposite wall. And somehow—as Lewis's narrator explains—that vision in the mirror is both the same and not the same as what you've just seen. It's the same, and yet it is "deeper, more wonderful, more like places in a story you have never heard but very much want to know."[23] That's how the new Narnia is. Every part of it looks "as if it meant more."[24] Old Professor Digory tries to explain that this is exactly what they should have expected when he proclaims, "It's all in Plato!"[25] Plato proposed the idea that our world is just a shadow of a truer, more real world of ideal thoughts and forms. Lewis offers mythic agreement when he has Aslan refer to our world as mere "Shadowlands."[26]

Two of the works on Tumnus's bookshelf show us that what is myth in our world is common fact in Narnia; the other two show us that common fact on Earth is regarded as myth in Narnia. These unusual opposites reveal something of C. S. Lewis's thought about myth: myth has connections to reality and truth; its content is not mere fantasy, but includes the possibility of real knowledge of the nature of things, including the truth that reality is made up of many more levels, natural and supernatural, than we see just in this universe. As we turn to look at the specific book titles in Tumnus's library, we will see Lewis work out these and other ideas with even greater detail and insight.

Part II
Narnian Reality, Terran Myth

Now we turn to the books proper, first considering those two titles in which what is myth in our world is reality in Narnia: *The Life and Letters of Silenus* and *Nymphs and Their Ways*.

CHAPTER FOUR

The Life and Letters of Silenus

Those of us who have seen Disney's *Fantasia* might remember a segment that features centaurs and other creatures from Greek mythology. In one scene, a portly, red-faced, clearly drunk fellow in a toga comes riding in on a donkey. That is old Silenus, at least one version of him. The first title in Tumnus's library is *The Life and Letters of Silenus*—but who is Silenus, and why would Tumnus care about him?

In Greek and Roman mythology, Silenus is something of a sidekick to Dionysus, or Bacchus,[1] so let's consider this god first. Lewis tells us that if the classical poet Ovid had written an ironic little book called the *The Art of Getting Drunk* (as he'd written *The Art of Love*), it would have starred the god Bacchus.[2] Nor does the god's reputation improve in medieval thought. In Statius, he becomes nothing more than the personification of drunkenness;[3] Lewis wrote of him in the same way.[4] Still, Bacchus is a little more complex than this, even in Lewis's writings. Bacchus is a fertility god, especially associated with the vine; by being the god of wine, he also becomes the god of revelry to the point of divine ecstasy. Lewis tells us of a "Bacchanalian spirit"[5] in his massive *English Literature in the Sixteenth Century*. There he cites *Bacchus' Bounty*, a text that describes the god, who "from a muddie muse so cleared up his cherry-like countenance that the majestie of his nose seemed as the beames of the sunne shining

along the Coastes of Archadie."⁶ In other words, the redness of
Bacchus's drunken face shined like the glory of the sun!

I used to describe Bacchus to my students as the "party god."
Lewis once wrote of how his friend Owen Barfield had been
making wine; when it was ready, they were thinking of having
a festival in Bacchic style at Barfield's house (a family-friendly
version) for which Lewis would write the poetry.⁷ But Lewis
wouldn't have us make light of this mythic figure. In his essay
"The Psalms," he draws a parallel between Psalm 96—in which
the earth and sky are glad, fields are joyful, and trees rejoice
before God because He's coming to judge the earth—and Greek
invocations of the god of wine and divine ecstasy: "At the pros-
pect of that judgement which we dread there is so much revelry
as a Pagan poet might have used to herald the coming of Dionysus."⁸ Jubilation and revelry, yes—but also danger and judg-
ment. Lewis reminds us that, when the Greeks wrote tragedies,
they did so in honor of Dionysus.⁹ Euripides' classic *The Bacchae*
tells us what happens when we ignore the power of the god: he
draws the women out of the city of Thebes in wild, hypnotic
trances and turns them into raging animals; they literally tear
apart their king, Pentheus, who has refused to honor Dionysus.

The predominant story of Bacchus's birth suggests this idea
of dangerous divine power: Zeus impregnates Semele; Hera,
Zeus's wife, finds out and tricks Semele into making Zeus
promise to appear to her in all his divine glory; when he reluc-
tantly gives in, Semele is burned to ash, but the divine child in
her womb survives; Zeus sews the preborn Dionysus up in his
thigh until he is ready to be born. The death of Semele through
exposure to the divine glory is echoed more than once in the
writings of C. S. Lewis. In describing God's method of reaching
down to man in myth that is also truth, the mystical voice of
God in *Pilgrim's Regress* tells the hero, John, that He purposely
chose to appear under this veil, explaining why He made our
senses and imaginations: that we might be able to see the face of

God and live. Then the divine voice reminds John of the pagan story of Semele.[10] She died because she encountered the raw, unveiled power of the god. Lewis suggests that God veils from man the absolute ideals of heavenly knowledge so we can see His truth but not be overwhelmed by it—so we can experience God without dying from contact with His pure essence. Much (though not all) of the knowledge God speaks to us He offers to our imaginations through story and myth.

The destructive power of divine glory is also a theme in *Till We Have Faces*. Psyche is married to a god (Cupid) who will not let her look upon him in the day nor by lamplight at night. When her sister Orual manipulates Psyche into breaking this command, her life is ruined and she faces untold suffering for years to come. Orual herself encounters the power of the divine when she enters a vision that takes her into the sacred land of the gods. There she approaches the immortal rams whose fleece is gold, and they turn and rush upon her. As they draw near, they become a wall of solid but living gold that knocks Orual flat and tramples her under hoof. But even in the terror and torment of that moment, she realizes that what the rams are doing to her isn't out of anger but out of joy, and she speculates that the "Divine Nature wounds and perhaps destroys us merely by being what it is," and to confuse this with the wrath of the gods is like believing a fly swept down a river was killed because the raging flood was angry with it.[11]

The danger of divine glory is also a scriptural image. When Moses asked to see God's glory, the Lord shielded Moses in the cleft of a rock as He passed by—"for no one may see me and live"—so that Moses got just the merest peak at God's coattails.[12] Imagine a glory so intense, a beauty so wonderful that it's terrible; it puts a whole new twist on the expression *drop-dead gorgeous*. Eventually Moses's continued exposure to the divine presence made his own face glow with that glory and become so terrible to the people that Moses had to start wearing a veil.[13]

In *The Lion, the Witch and the Wardrobe*, Aslan is described as appearing both good and terrible.[14] In *Out of the Silent Planet*, Lewis's hero, Ransom, experiences deadly glory as he flies through the heavens. The light of the sun shining upon his spaceship is tyrannical,[15] but fills him with energetic life.[16] He knows if that light were to break through the ship's thin shell it would kill him; however, to him it seems not so much death but life that is waiting outside, a life that would kill him only by its excess, not because of any malice: "To be let out, to be free, to dissolve into the ocean of eternal noon, seemed to him at certain moments a consummation even more desirable than their return to Earth."[17]

Again in *Till We Have Faces,* not only does Orual encounter the divine goats that trample her under hoof as they run, borne on by overwhelming, supernatural vitality, but she further faces the divine beauty at the novel's end when the god, Cupid, comes to her and makes her beautiful.[18] It's an incarnation of a major Lewis theme, one best explained in his most famous sermon, "The Weight of Glory." In describing our longing for God's glory and beauty, Lewis writes that we not only want to see it, but also want to be remade in it: "the poets and the mythologies know all about it." It's not enough for us just to see beauty—as wonderful as it is, we want "to be united with the beauty we see, to pass into it, to receive it into ourselves, to bathe in it, to become part of it,"[19] even if, as Ransom suggests, it kills us.

And so this is the symbolism of Bacchus in C. S. Lewis: Bacchus is what happens when the wild fury of God's love and glory enters the world of men.

Well, what about Silenus then? After all, the book on Tumnus's shelf is about him, not Bacchus. In some versions of the story, especially the one portrayed by Lewis in *Prince Caspian*, Silenus is the drunken attendant of Bacchus who rides a donkey and is an expert musician.[20] He regularly accompanies the god along with his maenads—nymphs, essentially—and joins in the wild dance of plenty. However, in other versions of the story, Silenus is himself a satyr and a wise mentor who tutors Bacchus.[21]

Tumnus shows us the interest he has in all of these sylvan creatures as he brings them into the wonderful stories he tells Lucy of life in the forest in the times before the White Witch, of ages past when nymphs of the wells and dryads of the trees would dance with the fauns at midnight; when Silenus would join them in the summers, riding on a rotund donkey, sometimes even accompanied by Bacchus, who would make the streams "run with wine instead of water."[22] Now, though, neither Bacchus nor Silenus has been seen since the coming of the witch's winter.

There will be more to say of these amazing characters when we discuss *Prince Caspian* at length, but I think we can explain the significance of *The Life and Letters of Silenus* on our favorite faun's bookshelf with only a little more information. One obvious point is that Silenus and Bacchus represent a time of joy now lost to the creatures of Narnia—especially the nature creatures like Tumnus, whose celebrations belong to spring and summer. But why a book on Silenus, when Bacchus seems the more important of the two?

The first reason may be that Silenus was around more in the old days. In Tumnus's memories of those long-ago summers, Silenus was a regular visitor; Bacchus himself would only come around "sometimes." Second, as I mentioned above, Silenus is sometimes a satyr himself. If so, then the familial relationship between Tumnus and Silenus is significant, since fauns and satyrs are closely connected and even interchangeable in their myths. Think about the stone lion in the witch's castle who, once he was awake, is excited to be associated with Aslan the great lion: "Did you hear what he said? *Us Lions.* That means him and me."[23] Tumnus might have felt very much the same way toward Silenus (at least until Lewis made Silenus into a little drunken man in *Prince Caspian*). For Tumnus to read about

Silenus would be to learn of someone like himself, only magically greater. There is, finally, the fact that Silenus is sometimes the wise tutor of Bacchus. This would explain why Tumnus has a book on Silenus's life and letters. Silenus is the smart one in the Bacchus–Silenus duo—he's the only one who would bother to write any letters and the only one having something to say worth putting on paper (or maybe parchment). Bacchus wouldn't sit still long enough to reflect on anything or take the time to write it down.

A few more notes: In a letter of 1947 (two years before he wrote *The Lion, the Witch and the Wardrobe*), Lewis suggested that pagan religions were closer to the truth than Eastern ones: "The man who rushed with the Maenads on the mountains to tear and eat the beast which also was the god [Bacchus] . . . that is far nearer the truth than Hinduism."[24] In an alternate version to the birth story of Bacchus, Zeus begets the god through Persephone. Hera, again, is angry and arranges to have the Titans attack the child; they kill, dismember, and eat the boy's flesh. Only his heart survives, which is swallowed by Zeus and then its essence transferred to Semele.[25] The parallels with Christ are fascinating: Bacchus is a resurrection god whose flesh is torn. In his rites, the animal sacrifice is torn apart and eaten, and in that ritual the animal becomes the god—Dionysus might as well have said to his followers, "Do this in remembrance of me." Admittedly, the cross represents an end to animal sacrifice, while this sacrificial need continues in the Bacchanalia. Yet the parallels still persist: wine, intimately tied to Bacchus, also becomes central to the Christian sacrament of communion.

Now talk of comparative religion might raise a red flag for some Christians, especially since atheists often use such parallel references to argue against Christianity. But for Lewis the opposite is true: In *Miracles*, he writes that God has given us the vine as a blessing; essentially, "He is the reality behind the false god Bacchus."[26] And in his essay "Miracles," Lewis says that God is the one who made grapevines and taught them to draw water up through their roots and, with the light of the sun, to turn the water into grapes, whose juice can be fermented into wine. Since the time of Noah, God has been turning water into wine, but people fail to see it. They either associate the process with a finite god—Bacchus or Dionysus—or, in modern times, they give it over to chemical and material causes. But, Lewis says, "when Christ at Cana makes water into wine, the mask is off."[27] Later in the same essay, Lewis writes that when Christ performed miracles of wine, bread, and healing, he "showed who Bacchus really was."[28] This is part of the reason that Bacchus shows up in *Prince Caspian.* Aslan is there to do a work of which Bacchus is an image. It's just that what is only myth on earth is real in Narnia. On earth, Bacchus is a picture of an idea. In Narnia, he's a living expression of it. But, upon his appearance in *Prince Caspian,* there is no question who is in charge. It's Aslan.

Finally, Bacchus and Silenus represent right pleasures—at least in Narnia. Christianity is often falsely tagged as a "kill-joy" faith. It's looked at as a religion of *no*'s and refusals, of asceticism and the rejection of pleasure for the sake of taking up one's cross. But as the demon Screwtape reminds his student Wormwood, God is, at heart, a hedonist: "He has filled His world full of pleasures. There are things for humans to do all day long without His minding in the least."[29] Bacchus and Silenus appear in Narnia because pleasure is not the enemy of God. Worldliness may be, but joy is not. On the contrary, "Joy is the serious business of heaven."[30]

CHAPTER FIVE

Fauns Are from Mars, Nymphs Are from Venus

Nymphs Proper

As we turn to *Nymphs and Their Ways,* let's first remember that nymphs are female; their closest male counterparts are actually satyrs and fauns. So basically, nymphs are the female sylvans with whom male sylvans—that is, a faun like Tumnus—would want to spend some quality time. In this sense Tolkien was right: *Nymphs and Their Ways* is very much concerned about the love life of a faun.[1]

Generally speaking, nymphs have a bad reputation in classical mythology. When he was still a teenager, Lewis was working on a poem on the mythic story of Hylas. Lewis tells us that, in the Argonautica, a poor mortal named Hylas is dipping his pitcher into a nymph's stream; catching him round the neck, she pulls him down to drown.[2] This is apparently a commonly nymph-ish thing to do and another reason Tumnus needs to brush up on "their ways."

This negative reputation continues past the classical age into the medieval and Renaissance eras. Writing about Christopher Marlowe's version of "Hero and Leander," Lewis describes a fantastical world where handsome boys could never be safe drinking from a natural spring because the water nymphs there would grab them and pull them to a drowning death.[3] In *The Discarded*

Image, nymphs are labeled as fairies—some of these fairies are wicked,[4] and sometimes they're specified as water creatures.[5] A great deal of attention was given to speculating on their place in the Christian cosmos;[6] yet, apparently, only Edmund Spenser did anything to preserve a positive image of these fairies when, in his day, they had come to symbolize only negative things.[7]

In Narnia, nymphs are "beautiful semi-divine maidens who live in a variety of natural habitats—trees, rivers, mountains, and so on."[8] Nymphs may be dryads, or wood nymphs; these are the spirits of trees (also connected to hamadryads) and referred to as "tree people"[9] or "tree-women."[10] There are also naiads, or water nymphs,[11] which are sometimes referred to as "well-women."[12] Interestingly, Narnia is referred to as the "country of the Waking Trees and Visible Naiads"[13] (among other creatures). But the terms, again, are somewhat interchangeable as indicated by the fact that Tumnus describes nymphs who lived in wells and dryads who lived in trees.[14]

In *The Lion, the Witch and the Wardrobe,* Tumnus tells us that nymphs dance with fauns[15] (hence, again, his interest in having a book about them), and they play stringed instruments at Aslan's pavilion.[16] Nymphs rise out of the river with Aslan's roar in *Prince Caspian.*[17] In *The Magician's Nephew,* four river nymphs—naiad daughters of the river god—bear the train of Queen Helen,[18] and the sons of King Frank and Queen Helen marry nymphs.[19] In *The Last Battle,* a tree spirit comes to warn King Tirian that trees are being cut down by men from Calormen, and then she dies before his eyes as her tree is felled.[20]

Gender and Incarnation: A Roundabout Lesson on Myth

Gender

Nymphs and Their Ways has something to teach us about the incarnational, even sacramental nature of myth, but it'll take a long detour down a forking side road to get there. After reviewing everything Lewis had to say on nymphs, I found myself with a series of questions related to gender: Why are nymphs and fauns counterparts to each other? Why are fauns the male version and nymphs the female version of a sylvan? Why are there no *faunettes* for the fauns or *menymphs* for the nymphs? Initially, I had some ambivalence toward seeking answers, because these aren't questions that Lewis himself addresses—at least, not directly. Also, it wasn't clear that these questions really had anything to do with Lewis's theory of myth. Eventually, though, I realized that examining questions of sylvan gender will take us, if in a roundabout way, to one of Lewis's key ideas on myth—an idea we might not get at in any other way.

In Lewis's thinking, gender is not merely physical, and physical bodies have spiritual importance. Lewis has often been attacked for his views on women, but the accusation of misogyny has been thoroughly answered;[21] I'm not going to take up that issue here, except to say that Lewis was neither a misogynist nor a feminist, where feminism is defined as a belief that there are no essential differences between women and men. His views on women are not what some today would call politically correct,[22] but they are born of a sacramental approach to sexuality.

One of the most famous Lewis quotes speaks to the comprehensive nature of his worldview. He says: "I believe in Christianity as I believe that the Sun has risen, not only because I see it, but because by it I see everything else."[23] Owen Barfield echoed this idea when he wrote, "Somehow what Lewis thought about everything was secretly present in what he said about anything."[24] Lewis believed what he did about gender because of what he believed about the entire universe: he believed it was part of a grand hierarchy of Being. We saw this while looking at Lewis's take on nature and supernature. He believed in an uncreated God above all created things, who then made both a supernatural and a natural order—the heavens and the earth of Genesis 1. He further believed it might be possible that there are natures stacked on top of natures in a massive hierarchy of

Being. But even if not, he believed that humankind was above the animals, the angels above us, and God above all. And it was because of his belief in a hierarchical creation, over which God is sovereign, that Lewis was suspicious of the idea of *equality*. In his essay "Equality," Lewis points out several problems with what we take today as an absolute virtue. One is that equality assumes an excess of human goodness. Most people believe in democracy because they think we are basically good and so deserve a participatory place in government.[25] The reason Lewis believes in democracy is because mankind is in a fallen state. He argues for democracy because all people are fallen, and therefore we shouldn't allow any one person too much political power. For Lewis, equality is not a good in the same way that wisdom or happiness is a good—that is, in and of itself. Equality is more like medicine. It's a corrective, not an ultimate goal. Medicine is desirable, but only when people are sick; perfect health is a far better thing.

This leads to a second problem with equality: when it is treated as a goal unto itself, it leads to the breeding of a mind that *demands* equality, that holds suspect any quality or person that smacks of superiority.[26] Lewis sees this reflected in an educational system that impedes the talented student for fear that his or her average classmates will suffer from the emotional trauma of low self-esteem.[27] In our own culture, it's economically visible in a drift toward entitlement and socialism; in education, it's apparent in the inflation of grades, in student/parent demands for passing grades; in youth sports, in the awarding of trophies to every kid on the team, regardless of how they finished; and in entertainment, in the dumbing down of television and film offerings, along with the celebration of such mediocrity.

Lewis's third problem is that idealizing equality starves us of our *desire for inequality*. An idea like this seems utterly alien to our culture—who would want inequality? Lewis's answer is that we all do. Because we were made by a God who is over us, who claims His heavenly order to be a kingdom, He has built into us a desire for hierarchy—a desire to honor those above us. Lewis rejects political hierarchy because of human fallenness, but he celebrates the British success of eliminating such hierarchy while retaining a monarchy, because the monarchy reminds us of and satisfies our need for inequality in the best ways. On this *need,* he is adamant: those who desire, who demand absolute equality for all, will not achieve it. If people aren't allowed to honor kings, they'll honor the icons of materialism, vainglory, and popular culture instead. Hierarchy is part of our spiritual nature; just as the physical body hungers to be fed, so the spiritual self demands the same. If we keep it from healthy food, it will simply eat poison.[28]

Though gender is a more complex issue for Lewis than the relationship between husbands and wives, he applies the danger of equality very specifically to marriage. Men, he says, have abused the power they've had over women to the point that equality may, for wives, be considered an ideal. But taking up an argument he gleaned from a book by Naomi Mitchison,[29] Lewis then says that, while legal equality, especially in marriage laws, should be pursued without reservation, there comes a point at which not only consent to inequality, but a delight in it becomes "an erotic necessity." According to Mitchison, women obsessed with the absolute good of equality in marriage become resentful of their husbands' embrace, and marriages are ruined as a result. Lewis laments that the modern woman is told by Freud that sexual fulfillment is the chief need of the psychological self, but then she is told by the feminist not to give in to "that internal surrender which alone can make it a complete emotional success."[30]

In our day, the typical reaction to this statement might be sympathy for any woman who ever got stuck in a marriage with Lewis. But anyone who has read a good biography on Lewis and his wife, the author Joy Davidman Gresham, will know that a miserable marriage was the last thing Joy had with her husband. As we explore them further, regardless of how we might judge them for ourselves, Lewis's thoughts on gender are surprising, neither stereotypically chauvinistic nor simplistic.

Using Mitchison's ideas, Lewis takes up the problem of equality and marriage in *That Hideous Strength* in an encounter that also illustrates a distinction that Lewis develops between physical and spiritual genders. When Jane Studdock meets the Director (Elwin Ransom, the hero of the previous space journey books), her nearly broken marriage becomes a subject in a conversation that includes her belief that love means equality and that all people are equal in their souls.[31] Ransom disagrees, turning to Lewis's medicine metaphor as well as noting the connection between obedience, humility, and erotic necessity.[32] Ransom does not, however, make any blanket statement that all women should obey all men, nor even that wives should always be in the position of obedience to husbands. Instead he says that the relationship is much more like a dance and that this is especially so because the roles between men and women are constantly changing.[33]

What Ransom does seem to insist on, though, is that "rule" is a masculine activity and "obedience" a feminine one. As she continues her journey of spiritual growth, Jane comes to realize that her conception of the spiritual world—the supernatural world—has been one of negation, of seeing it essentially as *unlike* the natural world. She had thought of it as a place where differences gave way to sameness, which meant also that sexual differences disappeared. But late in the novel she begins to realize that differences may be greater at higher levels in the hierarchy of Being, not less; that this might include differences in gender;[34] and that the quality of the masculine from which she had recoiled in marriage was not merely to be found in men, but in that which is higher. To this Ransom agrees, adding that Jane cannot avoid the masculine. Though she might have es-

caped the *male* had she not married—since the male is only biological—she and all other souls cannot avoid that transcendent
something that is even more masculine than what we encounter
on earth; it is something that requires an even deeper level of
surrender.[35] Jane's problem, says Ransom, has been the sin of
pride. It has been masculinity itself to which she has taken of-
fense: "the loud, irruptive, possessive thing—the gold lion, the
bearded bull—which breaks through the hedges and scatters the
little kingdom of your primness. . . . But the masculine none of
us can escape. What is above and beyond all things is so masculine that we are all feminine in relation to it."[36] The four elements we've covered in Lewis's theory of gender all appear in
this passage: that gender is born of a hierarchy in Being; that
a desire for equality can turn to pride and thus ruin the dance;
that gender is not merely biological, but transcendentally spiritual; and that, as such, one of the spiritual qualities of the masculine is rule, for which the feminine counterpart is obedience.
But, again, these are not qualities of men and women, offered
as proof that all men should rule and all women obey. They are
qualities of the masculine and feminine.

Twice in his fiction Lewis emphasizes the idea of gender as
spiritual and transcendent, not merely natural or biological. In
Perelandra, Ransom meets the Oyarsas (the governing angels) of
Mars and Venus. They appear to him in several forms, but the
final one is one most like his own. However, though these bodily
appearances are naked, they are free from normal human sexual
characteristics. At the same time Ransom can tell the difference
between them, and this difference is rooted in gender on a spiritual level. Ransom tries to describe it: he says Malacandra (Mars)
is akin to rhythm, while Perelandra (Venus) is more like melody.
Mars gives the appearance of holding a spear in his hand, while
Venus's hands are open with her palms facing Ransom. And
Lewis writes that, in this vision of the two Oyéresu, Ransom is
able to see what gender really means. But how to explain this?

The narrator notes with surprise that various languages make the same inanimate objects masculine or feminine in their tongues. Why, he wonders, do we make mountains masculine and certain trees feminine? It isn't just an act of projection; in fact, it's the reverse. It is because gender is in fact a "more fundamental reality than sex." Sexual differentiation is just the application to physical life of a "fundamental polarity which divides all created beings." The physical sexes are but one of many things in creation that have gender; there are realities in which the masculine and feminine may be encountered, but in which the distinction between male and female are without meaning. Ransom can see this in the apparent forms of the angelic beings before him—though they are sexless, the Oyarsa of Mars is not male but is masculine, while the Oyarsa of Venus is not female but is feminine.[37] The narrator goes on to describe Mars as seeming to always look outward like a guard on his watch, looking out for danger, while Venus's gaze is inward and veiled but looking to abundance and life.[38] Lewis implies that these qualities are spiritual ones—aspects of masculinity and femininity in the supernatural order.

In *That Hideous Strength*, Lewis speculates on the possibility that gender is an even greater quality of creation than we can comprehend. In describing the descent of the Oyarsas to Earth, he says Mercury, Venus, and Mars hold in their aspects "those two of the Seven Genders which bear a certain analogy to the biological sexes and can therefore be in some measure understood by men."[39] But the Oyarsas that were about to descend would possess genders which human beings could not comprehend.

I don't know that Lewis literally believed in more than two genders, but what's certain is that he believed that gender is spiritual. Yet just as Lewis would emphasize this idea, which many in our day would find shocking (believing gender to be a social construct), he would almost turn the tables on us by suggesting that physical gender is incarnationally tied to spiritual gender, that men are masculine, body *and* soul, and women feminine in both as well. Or put it this way: if Lewis believed gender was transcendent, so that there were times when men and women could even exchange roles, why would he then argue that there are real gender differences between men and women, differences that can prove role defining?

For Lewis, gender represents qualities that, on a spiritual level, are different. In our culture, even where feminism has been influential for some time, I suspect that we still tend to associate women with the heart and men with the head—women with feeling and men with logic. Interestingly, however, Lewis allegorizes reason in *The Pilgrim's Regress* in the form of a powerful, warrior woman,[40] a virgin warrior who is not married to "any particular worldview, but strikes down errors of logic, wherever they are found."[41]

Still, gender does indicate difference, and Lewis does not divorce it entirely from its corresponding biological sex. He believes men and women have more than biological differences. In his essay, "Modern Man and His Categories of Thought," he writes that the glory of the female mind is intensely practical and concrete, while the glory of the masculine mind is a "disinterested concern with the truth for truth's sake," with things that are cosmic and metaphysical.[42] A claim like this is likely to result in Lewis being labeled old-fashioned today, if not misogynistic; however, he does qualify his thoughts by noting that there are exceptions,[43] he does assign Reason to be a feminine figure in *The Pilgrim's Regress,* and he had many women friends with whom he shared the highest intellectual discourse.[44]

Another difference between men and women has to do with their attitudes toward the home and the community at large. Lewis claims that women tend to be more oriented toward the rights and protection of the family, and men toward the place of the family in the world around them.[45] In *The Screwtape Letters* Lewis suggests men and women have very different understandings of what it means to be unselfish.[46]

Besides believing there are essential differences between men and women, Lewis believes there are role differences as well. Following scripture, he argues that "headship" belongs to the husband in a marriage.[47] But Lewis's fullest statement on differing roles is to be found in his essay "Priestesses in the Church?" Lewis begins this essay, strangely enough, by suggesting there are limitations to reason and common sense,[48] but then takes up the common-sense arguments for having priestesses in the Anglican Church. He contrasts those sensible people who see the good in these arguments with those who intuit something wrong in them. This intuition, Lewis admits, cannot be argued from a history of the oppression of women in the church. Consider the Blessed Virgin in the Middle Ages—she was all but deified, and yet there was never a call for female priests. Then there is the existence of preachers or prophetesses in biblical times (as in Acts 21:9).[49] Puzzled by the resistance (including his own) to the idea of priestesses, Lewis next clarifies the nature of the priestly office, which is to be a representative of us to God and of God to us. It is with this second office that Lewis has a problem. He does not believe a woman can be in a priestly position of representing God to us.[50]

He makes this argument by considering it in reverse. Think about the ramifications of setting aside the argument that a "good woman can be like God," and begin by saying that "God is like a good woman." Perhaps we could start calling God our Mother in heaven. Perhaps it wouldn't have mattered at all if the Christ had come into the world as a woman instead of a man. Perhaps there is nothing wrong with reversing the imagery and saying the church is the bridegroom and Christ is the bride. Lewis argues that, if Christians were to embark down such a path, they would be taking up a different religion. There have certainly been goddesses and priestesses in religions through-out history, but these religions are characteristically very different from Christianity. Furthermore, if scripture is inspired, then the masculine imagery used of God is not arbitrary. This is as clear in poetry as in any religious argument. "Image and apprehension" cleave closely together, says Lewis; they represent an "organic unity" that common sense can't just set aside.[51]

Here he comes to the mystery of sexuality. "One of the ends for which sex was created was to symbolise to us the hidden things of God." It's something doubters may call irrational, but something believers call suprarational. All people, in relationship to God, are feminine.[52] This is part of the mystery; for that reason, only a man can take up the office of representing God before mankind—as a priest. If priests throughout the centuries have done a bad job of it, it is because they haven't been masculine enough. In other words, the problem of a bad husband cannot be fixed by reversing the roles. In dealing with the church, we are not just dealing with the male and the female on natural levels, but with what they "shadow," what they represent of supernatural realities beyond our understanding. Here we see Lewis concluding with a limitation on reason: Gender is housed in a mystery. It is more than biology; it is a spiritual reality. We don't know enough to play around with it. While Lewis does not eliminate leadership roles for women in a church (he recognizes preaching and prophesying), he does eliminate one: that of priest. And he does it based on the mystery of gender.

Lewis's view of gender is not feminist, but neither is it cartoonish or stereotypical. In *That Hideous Strength*, Lewis gives us the character of Fairy Hardcastle, who leads a secret police and bears the most cliché marks of everything Lewis found wrong with any kind of extreme feminism: mannish behavior, immodest dress, hunger for power, sex used as a weapon (along with a dose of sexual deviance).[53] If we were to contrast the Fairy with Ransom, we could easily argue that Lewis's imagining of a modern woman is unfair. But Fairy Hardcastle is *not* Ransom's counterpart. Her opposite in the novel is Grace Ironwood. Grace is in a leadership position at St. Anne's. She is a mature, intelligent woman, whose role in the actions of the story is significant.[54] She represents feminine strength. Conversely, Ransom in this novel and Sarah Smith in *The Great Divorce* offer us a fine comparison in regard to beauty, a quality that we normally associate with the feminine. Ransom's form is so attractive, it captivates Jane completely.[55] Of Sarah Smith's beauty, Lewis writes that men who looked upon her somehow became her paramours, but in a way that only made them love their own wives all the more.[56] Perhaps the best example of Lewis's complex view of gender is to be found in the final line of his obituary for Dorothy Sayers, where he thanks God for "her richly feminine qualities which showed through a port and manner superficially masculine."[57]

But still we haven't gotten an answer out of Lewis: If gender is spiritual, why argue real differences in type and roles between men and women? I think Lewis's answer is to be found in his understanding of the importance of incarnation. Simply put, Lewis believed in a marriage between body and soul—that human beings are not just physical, or just animal, but we are incarnated souls: souls inhabiting flesh; therefore, our gender is *not* merely biological, but *neither* is it merely spiritual. Our bodies and souls share a gender that is visible in our physical sexuality.

Incarnation

Incarnation is a significant idea in Lewis's thought. For example, where most Christians would emphasize the miraculous importance of Christ's Resurrection, Lewis refers to the Incarnation of Christ as the "grand miracle." That God became a man is the core miracle claimed by Christianity, and all other miracles prepare for it, manifest it, or result from it.[58] All of reality hangs together on the significance of the Incarnation, like the missing chapter from some ancient book that makes the rest of the book make sense.[59] The pattern that the Incarnation represents of descending and ascending, of death and rebirth, is the very pattern of nature itself,[60] a pattern sufficiently ingrained on the imaginations of humanity as to appear in myth around the world—in the stories of Adonis or Osiris, for example.[61] Christ is the fulfillment of that myth, a myth that understands the incarnational quality not just in Christ, not just in man, but in all of nature too. The myths of the nature-gods—Bacchus, Venus, and Ceres—are a type of the work God has been doing in nature all along. Therefore, neither Judaism nor Christianity professes the belief of many anti-nature religions that nature is either an illusion or a mistake, that to exist on a finite level is evil, and that the solution to this illusion, mistake, or evil is for all things in nature to return to God by some process of annihilation.[62] Neither is God merely another pagan nature-god. For this reason, the Jews were constantly warned against worshipping the nature-gods of those around them.[63] God is the author of nature—transcendent above it, but also immanent in it. This is the pattern expressed in nature and in the Incarnation: God descends in order to reascend. He dwelt among us and, in doing so, began a process by which all nature would be redeemed.

This is a shocking idea to much of the philosophy and religious thought of the world, but while other religions and philosophies (such as Buddhism or Gnosticism) condemn our physical nature, Christianity only calls for the correction of our nature; it does not, as Plato does for example, reject the physical self.[64] In fact, what separates Christianity from other religions is this very point: "it does not allow one to exclude or reject matter."[65] The Incarnation represents the coming of God into matter, and once God enters into a union with nature, He will not leave it, not even at the Ascension, so that nature itself must eventually be divinely glorified.[66] God intends to build a new nature for us, one that will include matter, space, time, and our senses[67] because we will be living there in new, glorified, but physical bodies.

Christ, nature, but also people. Humanity is God's most incarnational creation. We are composite creatures—natural organisms living in symbiosis with supernatural souls; we are matter and spirit both; prior to the Fall, that spirit was in complete harmony with its physical self, like the harmony between a king and his country, people and their homes, a family and its pets, or the human and equine parts of a centaur.[68] Incarnation is our natural state. Lewis finds proof of this truth in two unlikely facts: that people make crude jokes and are uncomfortable with corpses and ghosts.[69] Bathroom humor proclaims we are animals who find our animal nature funny. Why would we do that unless we were also spiritual? Lewis doubts that dogs see anything funny about being dogs, nor angels anything funny about being angels. We also fear both corpses and ghosts; perhaps this is because we intuitively know that bodies aren't meant to be without their spirits, nor spirits without their bodies. Mankind's uniqueness in the universe arises from the truth that, of all creation, we are the only incarnational creatures—the only beings of both spirit and flesh, a reality that God participated in at the "grand miracle" and one that Lewis believes God celebrates in us. In *Letters to Malcolm,* he tells us that, without our bodies, a vast area of the glory expressed by God would go without praise. Lewis is referring to creation as we perceive it with our senses. Animals can't appreciate like we can—nor can angels, who are pure minds, able to understand tastes and colors in one sense, but missing what we know by our palates and retinas. Lewis suspects that the beauties we encounter in God's creation are a secret between Him and us alone. It may be a reason God made us like he did and why the Christian doctrine of bodily resurrection is so important.[70]

The resurrection of the body means that people were meant to live eternally in an incarnated state. This amalgam of flesh and spirit is quite simply what we are. As such, our spiritual qualities will have at least some connections to our physical qualities—as in the case of gender. I'm not sure exactly what it means for men to have a masculine soul or women to have a feminine one, and, as Lewis has written, the gender roles can be fluid and sometimes reversed. But gender is a spiritual quality, representing real difference, and it is incarnationally tied to physical nature. It is because he believed in incarnation, then, that Lewis believed that there are spiritual differences between men and women.

Myth

The primary goal of this chapter, however, has been to learn something new about myth. Earlier, I posed a series of questions related to sylvans and gender, including: Why are fauns the male version and nymphs the female version of a sylvan? If we could ask Lewis why such very different creatures are counterparts to each other, he might answer that they represent differences in gender on a spiritual level as applied to the qualities of nature that transcend its mere physical existence. Taking Lewis's statement about centaurs in *Miracles,* we might speculate that fauns—half man, half goat—represent this concept of incarnation: of spirit permeating matter. But if so, the nymphs seem to be the opposite. They are the spirits of trees and springs, stepping out of their physical forms. Like the fauns, they show that matter is permeated by spirit, but they show it by separation rather than by union. Or, perhaps, the stepping out of the spirit is a mere projection and not a disunion, as Lewis suggests in his poem "Conversation Piece,"[71] where a dryad's separation from her tree destroys her.[72]

At any rate, nymphs seem something of an opposite representation from fauns—they seem to be spirits stepping out of their forms, breaking the bond of incarnation. Like the fauns, they show us matter permeated by spirit, but they show it by separation rather than by union (or, again, perhaps it's not so much separation as projection.) As noted earlier, in *The Last Battle,* a tree spirit who is physically a long way off from its tree warns Tirian that her forest is being chopped down—she dies in front of the last Narnian king as her own tree is felled, perhaps suggesting there is no separation between tree and spirit.[73]

Perhaps rather than representing separation of spirit and body, nymphs represent the odd connection between them: spirit and body are not the same, and yet they are tied together in human beings. At night we dream of far-off places, but those places are physical ones—our spirits roam but among sensory worlds. We can think thoughts no animal on earth can manage—we can theorize the possibility of a fourth dimension of space. Conversely, tumors, or accidental brain damage, or the ravages of dementia can trap our intangible selves in our bodies without any recourse even to clear thought. Perhaps fauns represent a hard, masculine reality—an absoluteness of incarnation. Perhaps nymphs represent a fluid, feminine understanding—the tentative side of the relationship between body and soul. I don't know, and Lewis gave us no more than hints.

These issues about sylvan gender are ultimately unresolvable—really, they would be of only passing interest, except that our speculation finally puts us in a place to derive new insight on myth.

What is it that makes us doubt the veracity of mythic stories? The simple answer is that they aren't true—that is, they tell stories that didn't happen. If they didn't happen, what connection do they have to reality? What truth could possibly be learned from mythology? We've already seen how Lewis believes myth can be true apart from actions in history, but the relationship between myth and reality is made more complex by the Incarnation of Christ and therefore by the incarnational theme woven in and out of the creation.

On Perelandra, Ransom is coming to a realization—one that he is trying hard to avoid. As his intellectual battle with the Un-man continues, Ransom gets a strong impression that he is meant to put an end to the conflict through physical means. Some presence is telling him he has to fight and kill the demon-possessed man lest his constant temptations of the Eve of that planet finally succeed. But Ransom is reluctant, primarily because he's afraid. As an excuse he thinks to himself that the reduction of spiritual warfare to a mere fistfight would seem ridiculously mythological. But then he sees the truth: in his time on Mars, and even more so on Venus, Ransom had realized that the "triple distinction of truth from myth and of both from fact was purely terrestrial," belonging to a division in us between body and soul, which was a result of the Fall.[74] Ransom realizes that, even in our fallen world, this separation is not total, that the sacraments are a reminder of this truth, that the elimination of this division began at the Incarnation of Christ. In *Miracles,* Lewis looks to the day of our Resurrection into glory where we will see "fact and myth remarried."[75]

Here we learn that the Incarnation of Christ is a watershed moment: a place where fact (history) and myth come together. This is the central idea in one of Lewis's better known essays, "Myth Became Fact," first published late in 1944. In it Lewis takes up an epistemological problem (a problem of how human knowing works)—something I'll have more to say about later. In the essay, Lewis argues that our thoughts about reality are abstract, but our experiences of reality, though concrete, are particular, not universal; he believes that myth can connect us to supernatural reality—the universal reality above the world of our common experiences. It does this in ways that are not possible for either abstract thought or particular life experiences.

As Lewis puts it, "myth is the isthmus which connects the peninsular world of thought with that vast continent we really belong to. It is not, like truth, abstract; nor is it, like direct experience, bound to the particular."[76] In his metaphor, Lewis is saying that between the peninsula of thought and the continent of higher, supernatural reality, lies myth. Myth is the device that allows us to access the higher reality without reducing it to either abstract thought or mere experiential examples. Then Lewis makes his great statement on the coming together of reality and myth: "Now as myth transcends thought, Incarnation transcends myth. The heart of Christianity is a myth which is also a fact. The old myth of the Dying God, *without ceasing to be myth,* comes down from the heaven of legend and imagination to the earth of history. It *happens.* . . ."[77] Where the myths of other dying gods, such as Osiris or Balder, happen in no definitive point in history, the story of Christ happens in specific time under the governorship of a specific Roman ruler. And even though it has become a fact, the story miraculously remains a myth.

Lewis had little to say of nymphs, specifically. But in recognizing the gender difference between nymphs and fauns, we have been able to follow Lewis to an interesting end—through gender to hierarchy, to incarnation and the one myth that was also a fact. In chapter 3 we explored the possibility that myth might be real—that it might have some connection to our physical existence. Here, albeit taking a long way round, we've come to understand that myth is breathed in the Incarnation and that, at least one time in history, myth became fact.

CHAPTER SIX

Why Sylvan Myths Matter

Now that we've looked at the books in Tumnus's library in which Terran myth is Narnian reality, we can give some thought to drawing together what it all means in Lewis's thinking. Why does he bring classical mythology from Earth into Narnia? And why *these* mythical creatures in particular? Why the sylvans and Bacchus? The more pointed question might be: Was Lewis, as a Christian, right in doing what he did? In other words, what place should Christians give to these pagan creatures in our art and thought?

In *The Allegory of Love,* Lewis explains at some length why the pagan myths of the Greeks and Romans survived through the rise and dominance of Christianity. The gods were real to pagan peoples, but, even before Christianity came along, the philosophers of the West began using the gods as symbols for the inner life, the mind of man. Lewis writes specifically that the end of the old pagan gods is in no way a result of the rise of Christianity. Instead, the end of pagan religion occurred when polytheism met philosophy: monotheism arises naturally in polytheistic cultures wherever speculative thought and leisure exist.[1]

Once the minds of the philosophers—the great thinkers—have embraced monotheism, the next question becomes what are they to do with the gods of popular religion? Their answer, both in philosophy (as far back as the Stoics) and poetry is that the gods come to be viewed as embodiments of various aspects of the divine. The abstract attributes of the one divine power become personified in the individual gods of a pagan pantheon[2] (Cupid, for example, becomes the living symbol of divine love). But they do not remain personifications alone. Eventually they develop into the complex spiritual allegories of medieval and Renaissance Christian theologians and poets, the Neoplatonists, Dante, and Spenser.[3] Or else their reality—the reality of the semidivine creatures like fairies and fauns—becomes the stuff of theological speculation.

As we saw in *The Discarded Image*, they become a group of creatures called Longevai, which may or may not exist. If they do exist, they may exist somewhere between man and angel, or they may be actual demons in disguise. But the bottom line is that we have these stories from classical mythology because Christianity saw them as stories worth preserving. This is true not only of early Christianity and the myths of Greece and Rome, but of medieval Christianity as well. Much of what we have of Norse mythology was preserved through such works as the Icelandic Eddas, written in an age when Christianity was already well established in Europe and Iceland. In using pagan myth, then, Lewis is following a tradition that goes back to the roots of Christian practice and thought.

So what does Lewis convert these pagan sylvans into in Narnia? One major theme is made clear in *Prince Caspian*. They represent nature as a living, sentient entity, especially standing off against a view of progress that sees nature as a hindrance to human endeavor, one that must be overcome with hatchet, axe, and cement.

Upon conquering Narnia, the Telmarines begin a process of modernization that goes on for hundreds of years up to the events of *Prince Caspian*. At the time of the novel, they've built a bridge—a symbol of conquest and control—over the river at the fords of Beruna, chaining the river-god to that place.[4] And because the Telmarines have chopped down forests and defiled streams, the dryads and naiads of Narnia have fallen asleep.[5] The dance of the fauns that Tumnus so lamented during the hundred-year winter returns in *Prince Caspian,* and the young prince gets to participate in it.[6] Then the whole action of the novel revolves around two plots, not one. The first, the one readers tend to focus on, is the establishment of Caspian as the rightful king in Narnia, but the second is equally important: it is the restoration of Narnian nature herself—and therefore of every sylvan creature currently slumbering under the weight of so-called human progress. Restoring nature is as much (if not more) a part of this novel's plot as was restoring spring in the *Wardrobe.* Lucy begs the trees to wake up in *Caspian,* crying out to the dryads and hamadryads to come to her.[7] But they don't, not at first.

It's not until Aslan comes that the trees wake and move and bow and curtsy and shout the name of Aslan: birch-girls, willow-women, beeches, oak-men, elms, hollies, and rowans all pay homage to the lion.[8] Then, even more amazing, a curly haired youth appears accompanied by an old and very fat man on a donkey. He constantly falls off the donkey and shouts, "Refreshments!" and a romp ensues—for Bacchus and Silenus have returned to Narnia![9] Creatures all through the wood laugh and shout out, "Euan, Euan, eu-oi-oi-oi,"[10] which is a Greek cry, the first half representing another name for Bacchus, the second half an interjection[11] (like shouting, "Ba-bam!" in English). It's Lucy, then, who identifies Bacchus and Silenus, remembering that Mr. Tumnus told her about them long ago. Susan at once reminds us of the power and danger of this godling when she says she wouldn't have felt entirely safe around Bacchus and his wild women if Aslan hadn't been around.[12] Lucy agrees. It is Aslan, the true source of Bacchic power and pleasure, who governs the living personification of that power in the form of the wild boy and his wood-women. The pagan god answers to the true God, as Lewis believed was the case with ancient myth.

Trumpkin the dwarf describes the beauty, majesty, and even the fearful awe of the gathering of the trees against the army of Miraz: huge and beautiful creatures "like gods and goddesses and giants." Trufflehunter names these "the Dryads and Hamadryads and Silvans" and explains that Aslan has awakened them.[13] When the trees join the battle, the sound is like a wild, southwestern wind breaking over a high ridge "in full fury on an autumn evening."[14]

As the battle against the Telmarine army ensues, Aslan and his company of sylvans continue the fight to reclaim the land and the people's right balance with it. The great lion orders Bacchus to free the river-god from his chains,[15] which the boy does by making ivy grow up on the bridge and tear it apart. Now this isn't all that happens to restore a balance to things in Narnia— but let's save that last bit for a few moments, while we turn our attention to a parallel story.

In 1947, a few years before the writing of the Narnia books, Lewis wrote a poem entitled "Pan's Purge," in which he imagines a revolution by nature coming to England. In the poem he dreams that humanity has completely crushed nature beneath its feet, sterilizing the earth and causing the lion and unicorn to cry over the death of Pan.[16]

The animals continue to lament the loss of the god, until suddenly a change comes over them: sorrow fades and is replaced by anger as they cry out that Pan is not dead. Suddenly then the North Wind rises and draws his scimitar, coming in his full power to bring about mankind's doom.[17] So at the behest of Pan, nature rises up to bring about the destruction of industrializing humankind.

Lewis hated what so-called progress in England was doing to nature. In September 1914, he went to live with his new tutor (and favorite teacher), William Kirkpatrick, at his home in the village of Great Bookham, Surrey (a county in the south of England). Here Lewis describes his ideal world as a place of perfect rest that has been forgotten by time—that is, by progress—and he claims Great Bookham is such a place.[18] For Lewis, such time-forgotten refuges are natural places that mechanical progress stands ready to invade. He associates truest pleasures—what he calls "Pleasures of Appreciation"[19]—with the beauty of flowers in a garden; he adds that the person will be sorrowful who hears that a garden he enjoyed with special intensity has been demolished and replaced with a movie theater, an auto garage, or a highway.[20] Lewis's attitude here is reflected in the eco-destroying actions of his villains in *That Hideous Strength,* where the ultimate goal of those who stand against all goodness is to eliminate all objects of nature, from trees and birds to human bodies and physical reproduction.[21]

This attitude is equally present in the villainous misbehavior of two boys in the Narnia series. On his way to betray his siblings to the witch in *The Lion, the Witch and the Wardrobe,* Edmund tries to keep himself warm with the progressive plans he will institute upon being made king, these include the building of proper roads, the construction of a palace, procuring several cars, building his own personal movie theater, and mapping out the Narnian railway system.[22] Eustace suffers this same kind of attitude at the beginning of *The Voyage of the Dawn Treader.* This is not entirely his fault since his parents, who are modern, progressive people, have raised him to like animals most when they are dead and pinned on a display and to like only those books filled with information about grain elevators and foreign kids in modern, experimental schools.[23]

Personal letters also reveal Lewis's dismay. He laments that the country around his home is being destroyed by housing development,[24] and he worries that he may live long enough to see a time when the south of England has no real countryside left in it.[25] Sadly, progress continued to make things worse over the next three decades. In one letter, Lewis laments the loss of a beautiful "beechwood" to road construction near his home ("drat them") and concludes that inventing the internal combustion engine may have been worse than inventing the atomic bomb.[26] In contrast, he could still find moments of natural splendor in the wasteland his England was becoming. While he acknowledged in 1950 that foreigners might look at England as a single giant industrial complex, he writes that there are still spots of natural, unspoiled beauty to be found, even in areas heavy with industry—villages away from the main roads where things seem not to have changed in the last several centuries.[27] He also writes happily of finding that, though Oxford has been largely ruined by industrialization, his new teaching home of Cambridge, in the mid-1950s, was still wonderfully small—a place where he could get himself a real walk in the country any time he wanted to.[28] Still his grim prediction regarding the ultimate effects of progress is one of permanent encroachment leading ultimately to nothing less than a "universal suburbia."[29] Perhaps Lewis didn't merely write a poem on the purging of Pan, but a *prayer* for it.

All of this takes us to a second meaning for the sylvans in Lewis's thinking: they represent his rejection of a mechanistic view of nature—one that robs nature of meaning and its symbolism of abundance in life. At the end of their march of restoration in *Prince Caspian,* Aslan and company (and again Bacchus is instrumental) work to save not just nature but several individual people from a life of dullness and impotence. A girl is rescued from history lessons and a controlling teacher[30]—not because history is bad, but because the way it is taught under the Miraz school of history is dull and boring. Farm animals cruelly spent of their lives join Aslan's party and become rejuvenated again.[31] A man beating a boy with a stick is turned into a tree, and the boy saved in a burst of laughter.[32] Then, rather than a student saved from a teacher, a teacher is actually saved from her pigish, Eustace-like students.[33] Finally, an old sick woman in a cottage (who turns out to be Caspian's old nurse) is healed when Bacchus dips a pitcher into the well and draws up water that turns to wine for her to drink: "red as red-currant jelly, smooth as oil, strong as beef, warming as tea, cool as dew."[34] What we're seeing here, then, is this second theme that the sylvans represent. The forces of nature systematically defeat the forces of modernity, which kill the joy of people trapped in artificial constructs: a child abused by his father, a student by a teacher, a teacher by her students, an old woman by the walls of a rundown cottage and her own fading body—all this occurring among images of natural flora overwhelming man-made buildings.

In an essay entitled "The Empty Universe," Lewis writes of a trend in human thought that goes back to the beginnings of philosophy. He says the process by which humankind has come to know the universe, though complicated, is in one sense very simple. At first the cosmos appears to us to be filled with thought, life, all positive things—the trees are nymphs, the planets are gods, and mankind is "akin to the gods." But, as our knowledge increases, we begin to empty this fecund, jovial creation of its gods and spirits, of its "colors, smells, sounds and tastes," until the very same methods by which we emptied our universe of meaning begins to empty us as well. It turns out, according to the learned, that we were just as wrong to attribute "souls," "selves," or "minds" to the human animal as we were to attribute dryads and naiads to trees and springs. We personified the world, and, when we lifted the veil of ignorance from this activity, we found out that we were merely personifications ourselves. As dryads are only abbreviated symbols for what we know about trees, stupidly mistaken for some mysterious spirit above that knowledge, so human "consciousness" or the "mind" turns out to be nothing more than an "abbreviated symbol for certain verifiable facts about his behaviour."[35]

Lewis's last point here connects to the question posed in the book title on Tumnus's shelf: Is man a myth? In the progression of human thought to Lewis's day, it turns out that just as we have personified all things in nature, so do we personify man himself—we turn out to be impersonal machines, and everything

we thought about ourselves was a myth (or a "lie," as is the unfortunately more common meaning of the word *myth*). But Lewis's first point in "The Empty Universe" is what his sylvans stand
as a symbol against. The rise of science—or of "scientism"—has
stripped wonder, meaning, and even life from our view of nature. Recall the moment in *The Voyage of the Dawn Treader* when
Eustace, having learned that stars are living creatures, says that,
in our Terran universe, they're just big balls of fiery gas. Raman-
du's reply represents Lewis's response to the mechanization of
nature: Even in our world, "that is not what a star is but only
what it is made of."[36]

Lewis's sylvans symbolize his pushback against the trend of
reducing everything in nature to mere machinery. The world is
made flat, dull, and meaningless. Life loses all sense of wonder.
Spirit is removed from the world (because apparently spirit does
not exist). But maybe this is only because, like in Narnia, the
spirits have gone to sleep. And maybe Christians are as much
to blame for this as materialists. Consider, for example, what
Christ said to the Pharisees when they told Him to tell the crowd
not to shout that He was the coming king: "If they keep quiet,
the stones will cry out."[37] For Lewis (as for Christ), this statement was more than just hyperbole. But how many of Lewis's
fellow Christians really believe it—that the abundant life of God
is so intense that it could pour itself even into inanimate objects?
Maybe we fear falling into pantheism, but perhaps instead we
have given into the lie that the magic has gone from the world.

I've noticed, for example, that, Christian or not, people have a
tendency to talk about the "real" world—to use phrases like *that's
real* or *that's reality* or *time to go back to the real world*—always in
negative ways, as if reality equals the death of dreams, bad things
happening, and being predestined to little more than paying the
monthly bills. We've become like the child or the teacher or the
old woman in need of rescue at the end of *Prince Caspian*. This
dull, lifeless world is exactly the world that the Green Lady tries

to talk Eustace, Jill, Puddleglum, and Rilian into accepting in *The Silver Chair*. When they claim that the Overworld exists, she asks for proof, which they attempt to offer in the existence of the sun or of Aslan. But she counters these proofs with an old Freudian argument: that they are mere wish-fulfillment. The sun is merely their overblown conception of a lamp. Aslan is merely their false myth built from the actual existence of little cats.[38]

But then Puddleglum makes the heroic reply that if they have made up the beautiful world of nature in the land above, of the sun and the moon and of trees and grass, then that made-up world must be far more important than the so-called real world of the Green Lady's kingdom. If her dark pit is the only world, then it's a poor one, and they are just babies playing a game; however, "babies playing a game can make a play-world which licks your real world hollow."[39] Puddleglum concludes that he and his friends intend to leave the Green Lady's world and search for Narnia, and, though he fully expects they'll die in the search, it's a "small loss if the world's as dull a place as you say."[40]

Lewis's sylvans—especially his naiads and dryads—are nothing less than the dynamic symbols of a world of abundant life, of the personality that exists behind all living things, of a universe that is far more organism than machine. The sleeping trees in *Prince Caspian* have been put to sleep by modernity, by scientific materialism. Lewis's intention is to reawaken them.

That which the materialists fail to put to sleep, they tear apart and destroy. In his poem "Conversation Piece," written in the same year as *The Lion, the Witch and the Wardrobe*, a magician (who in Lewis's mind often stands for any group of scientists more interested in gaining power than knowledge) forces a dryad from her tree in order to talk to her. But the sudden disconnection of the spirit from her total existence with the earth overwhelms her, and she pines away and dies.[41] Similarly, in *The Abolition of Man*, Lewis writes that when man conquers nature, he ends up paying a stiff price for it: we don't look at trees as either things of beauty or as dryads when we're cutting them into posts. Perhaps the first woodsman did and felt guilty for the act of desecration. Perhaps Virgil felt the echo of the loss and so created an image of trees that bleed. But as trees became mere wood for construction, so the stars lost any association with divinity at the creation of telescopes, and agricultural gods who died and were reborn found no place in the fertile fields of modern husbandry.[42]

It seems strange that Lewis would celebrate pagan myths—but, again, it's because he believed they held kernels of truth. In his essay "Religion without Dogma?" for example, Lewis argues against a modern trend toward vague, spiritualized, or "minimal" religions. He doesn't think them strong enough. For him they hold no power. A "flag, a song, an old school tie"[43] would prove stronger. Pagan religions would prove stronger. Lewis—the devout Christian—writes that, instead of relying on a minimal religion, he would almost listen again to the drumbeat in his blood and join the maenads in singing; he writes of how happy are those who have been befriended by the gods and entered the mystic rituals, the dance throbbing with their heart as they join revelries with Dionysus on the mountainside.[44] And, Lewis concludes, he'd rather "be a pagan suckled in a creed outworn,"[45] quoting Wordsworth's poem, "The World is Too Much with Us":

The world is too much with us; late and soon,
Getting and spending, we lay waste our powers;—
Little we see in Nature that is ours;
We have given our hearts away, a sordid boon!
This Sea that bares her bosom to the moon;
The winds that will be howling at all hours,
And are up-gathered now like sleeping flowers;
For this, for everything, we are out of tune;
It moves us not. Great God! I'd rather be
A Pagan suckled in a creed outworn;

So might I, standing on this pleasant lea,
Have glimpses that would make me less forlorn;
Have sight of Proteus rising from the sea;
Or hear old Triton blow his wreathèd horn.[46]

Lewis's point (and Wordsworth's) is that, at least as pagans, we might look to the heavens and see fiery Helios driving his chariot across the sky; instead, we look up and see the sun—a big ball of gas.

Yes, Lewis loves the pagans. No vague spiritualized religion for him. He points out that, when the pagans went to worship Bacchus, they drank and got drunk.[47] Lewis doesn't make this point because he liked to drink (he did), but because the worship of Bacchus was a nature religion, the kind that shows us the key pattern in nature—death and rebirth[48]—a pattern revealed in the myth that would become fact: the story of Christ. Lewis calls such religion a clue or primary theme in the story of the universe.[49] This is because God constantly does what we see nature-gods doing. God is the true Bacchus, the true Venus. At the center of Christianity is the idea of sacrifice—remove that idea and both paganism and Judaism (as well as Christianity) lose all their meaning:

> Can one believe that there was just *nothing* in that persistent *motif* of blood, death, and resurrection, which runs like a black and scarlet cord through all the greater myths– thro' Balder & Dionysus & Adonis and the Graal too? Surely the history of the human mind hangs together better if you suppose that all this was the first shadowy approach of something whose reality came with Christ. . . . [50]

Even before he was a Christian, Lewis was being moved by pagan myth toward the existence of God: In an early poem called "Song," Lewis writes that faeries and satyrs and Tritons must exist or how could the so-called lifeless things of nature be anywhere near as beautiful as they are?[51] Dead atoms couldn't possibly stir the heart; instead, the beauty we see must be from spirits inhabiting those places, spirits that have been to heaven and seen the "bright footprints God."[52] This is not Lewis coming to a belief in God (that would come later). But, as he explains in a letter in which he references this poem, "perhaps there is a spirit behind the world . . . which we can nevertheless see in material things: an 'indwelling spirit behind the matter of the tree—the Dryad in fact.'"[53] Lewis didn't know it at the time, but he was on a journey toward finding God, and he was finding Him through pagan myths. Or, to put this another way: Lewis's near paganism was essential to his conversion to Christianity! He even said of himself in one letter that by almost believing in the pagan gods he came to believe in the God who is really there.[54] And, in the opening paragraph of his essay, "Is Theism Important?" he writes that he prefers pagans to modern man because the pagans are far more easily converted![55]

Lewis also held some very specific theoretical ideas about the nature of myth, which we'll explore further in the next section. Briefly, however, Lewis looked at the ancient myths as sources of what his friend Owen Barfield called "concrete" thought (and we'll have a lot to cover regarding this difficult concept); he also considered the implications rising from the question of whether or not the creatures of Greek myth actually existed. In his poem "A Footnote to Pre-history,"[56] for instance, Lewis speculates on the possibility that many of the mythic creatures we know were real. Adam and Eve encountered them in fear upon being cast out of Eden: dwarves, monopods (the precursors to the Dufflepuds), trolls, and giants—who all died later in Noah's flood. Lewis then suggests that we know of such creatures because their memory is passed down in a kind of collective unconscious through Eve. Memory reaches us so that we have heard of the existence of mythical creatures through her experience of them, an experience passed on to Seth while he was still in the womb, which has continued to echo in human minds down the ages.[57]

In "Is Theology Poetry?" Lewis uses fairies to exemplify the different imaginative pleasures we get depending on whether or not we believe them to be real. Here Lewis asks whether belief in a thing might prove an enemy to be enjoying it imaginatively. He concludes that, if we believe in a mythology, we will somewhat spoil it for purposes of imaginative or artistic enjoyment.[58] Lewis says something similar in his afterword to the third edition of *The Pilgrim's Regress,* regarding the strong sense of longing that was a source of his eventual conversion and that was aroused by reading classic myths. He writes that when Arthur Conan Doyle (of Sherlock Holmes fame) claimed he'd photographed a fairy, Lewis didn't believe it; however, the fact that Doyle had made the claim—the possibility of a fairy's existence—revealed to Lewis that, if Doyle had been right, the result would have been a chilling rather than a satisfying of the desire fairy tales had aroused in him. If the sylvans of forest myth were real, he says, the "Sweet Desire" that they invoke would disappear.[59]

Here Lewis hints at a lesson on myth we'll come to later: this "Sweet Desire" that he refers to, using such words as *longing, joy,* and *Sehnsucht* (a German word meaning a longing for some unobtainable thing), was aroused by myth and became a key factor in the process of Lewis's coming to Christ. For Lewis, the sylvans became a symbol of both the arousing of this longing and the glory of the invisible God piercing through to the visible world, which these mythic creatures helped reveal. But before we get to this lesson, we shift ground from the myths of Earth to the myths of Narnia. Among them, us.

Part III
Terran Reality as Myth in Narnia

In the next two works on the faun's bookshelf, Lewis uses the terms *legend* and *myth* in ways that were typical in his day: as referring to things questionable and untrue. Lewis himself had once believed the same thing, but his view changed radically. In part II of this study, we looked at book titles that showed that what was myth on Earth was reality in Narnia. *Men, Monks, and Gamekeepers* and *Is Man a Myth?* represent a total contrast: books in which Terran reality is Narnian myth. As such, they bring us to the point where we need to lay a more complete groundwork for exploring the nature of myth. So we will first examine Lewis's ideas on the origins and definitions of myth. Then we can look at Tumnus's books in light of what we learn.

CHAPTER SEVEN

Defining Myth

 Understanding myth requires trying to do two things at once: defining myth *and* discovering its origins. Young (and hotly atheistic) C. S. Lewis, for example, believed myths were nothing more than primitive inventions. He wrote to his friend Arthur Greeves that dryads and other sylvan creatures of classical myth were just a "development of the primitive savage idea that everything has a spirit (just as your precious Jehovah is an old Hebrew thunder spirit)."[1] A few months later he wrote that all the religions of the world, or "all mythologies to give them their proper name," are nothing more than human inventions, true as much of Christ as it is of the Norse god Loki.[2] He claimed that primitive humanity superstitiously supposed that all the evils they encountered in the world were the work of evil spirits that had to be kept at bay through the singing of songs and the making of sacrifices. More complex ideas were gradually attached to these nature spirits till they became envisioned as the old gods; as man became more refined, he attached moral good to these spirits. The teenage Lewis smugly added that this is knowledge that his friend Arthur should have heard before since it is the received scientific explanation for the development of religions.

Still, even though Lewis believed myth to be false, he loved it—had a great sympathy for it; he believed myths were beautiful.

Because of this duality—intellectual falsehood combined with imaginative beauty—Lewis almost thought myth a cheat. Thus, in his early poem, "The Satyr," he uses the doubled nature of the mythical creature to suggest both the desire the myth awakens and the disappointment of that desire. Though this satyr awakens the fairies to make music (a positive image), his legs are "shaggy" and "twisted" (a negative image).[3] His brow may be clear and the color of snow, but he has cloven feet.[4] And his temples may be lovely, but horns protrude from them.[5] In most stories, satyrs love chasing after nymphs. But this one has sad eyes, because he sees the futility of the chase, and does not follow the nymphs.[6] "Night," which is part of the same cycle of poems that "The Satyr" was published in, is similar in its lovely description of a magical wood, where fairies dance and call human beings to come into their country. Kings in ancient times found their way there, found beautiful fairy maidens to love, but only at a price. The idyllic poem ends with the warning that these ancient kings could not be saved.[7]

Lewis's ideas about myth began to change after he read Owen Barfield's *Poetic Diction*. In studying the history of language, Barfield came to the conclusion that myth represents a mode of thought common to ancient man, but one that modern man has lost. Lewis read *Poetic Diction* in thesis form in the mid-1920s; upon its publication a few years later, he became seriously interested in myth as an intellectual pursuit. What had been a source of imaginative pleasure for Lewis—myth—suddenly became something worth philosophical contemplation. Lewis indicates this new interest in a pair of letters he wrote to Barfield in 1928 after rereading *Poetic Diction*. In the first of these letters,[8] Lewis writes that he has just obtained a copy of Barfield's book, having learned of its publication from a poorly done review in the *Times Literary Supplement*. But Lewis is astonished by Barfield's content, and he's certain his second reading of *Poetic Diction* will result in his agreeing with the book far more than either

he or Barfield thought he would. The second letter was written to Barfield in June 1928. Lewis seriously argues the need for
a new word for describing the study of myth (since *mythology*
had already been applied to the myths themselves) and suggests
the word *mythonomy*. He demands that if Barfield's views about
myth are anywhere close to accurate, they'll need a really good
word for the study of myth before someone invents a "beastly
one."[9] The letter continues with several additional options such
as *mytho-logic* and *mythopoeics.*[10]

We've recently learned that Lewis didn't just mention the
study of myth in a few letters at this point in his life. He took a
passing crack at it in a fragment or pair of fragments that were
first published in 2015.[11] I discovered this text buried in the back
of a copy of a Lewis notebook at the Marion E. Wade Center.[12]
The letters above, along with a chart I've developed for mapping
out changes in Lewis's handwriting throughout his lifetime,[13]
allowed me to confidently date the text to 1928. I gave it the title
"Mythonomy," following Lewis's suggestion. The first half of
the fragment contrasts Zeus with Odin, focusing on the differences between a god who is immortal (Zeus) and one who can
die. But the second half of the "Mythonomy" fragment takes
up the theory of myth itself. In it, Lewis, for the first time in
writing, explores the origins of myth.

Lewis begins with the distinction between conscious and unconscious invention, offering the label "fiction" for the former.
As an example of the latter, Lewis imagines two children speculating about what happened to some characters in a story after
the tale is done. The story grows organically, with the children
offering and then accepting various details as their expansion
of the story develops.[14] But if the same children were asked to
stop guessing and consciously create a story instead, their in-
ventiveness might be utterly stifled, unless they are exceptionally
imaginative. It is "unavowed invention" that Lewis thinks might
be key to the process of myth-making—of the stories of Atli and

Gunther,[15] for instance, as they were teased out of their historical sources.

Lewis adds "happy errors" as another piece to the making of myths, along with the "reminiscent delusion," which, for example, causes an actual person who is nevertheless larger than life to appear in more places than possible. Here Lewis uses the example of the infamous Red Baron in World War I,[16] who too many claimed to have shot down and too many (including Lewis himself) claimed to have seen in the skies above them. And Lewis realizes that, just as the illustration of children inventing a story offers one root to the origins of myth, so do the conversations of soldiers in the field show another. The constant chatter about heroes and accomplishments on the battlefield (a chatter that mixes true memories with confused ones), along with the imagination's tendency to finish incomplete stories or add interest and intensity to what is otherwise not so powerful a tale—these, mixed together with some purposeful lies, all provide source material for the making of myths, the great epic tales of the past.

But then Lewis offers a glimpse of something larger, and this may be the first time he recognizes there could be more to myth than just human invention and lies: "The third element that goes to the making of epic is harder for us to understand. There is little in our modern experience that illuminates the mythical scenes and characters. Where do the dragons come from? The origin of myths[17] We must answer that we do not know."[18] Imagine C. S. Lewis making headway in his thoughts on the development of story-making and its transformation into myth-making, and then getting to this mysterious and unexplained third element and the question of where dragons come from. Suddenly he faces a yawning metaphysical chasm, one that he cannot yet cross. He had moved forward from atheism to a belief in spirit beyond the physical world, but from there he can get no further (not yet) and still cannot see where myth fits into his beliefs.

Lewis became a theist in 1930.[19] But the final step of his conversion to Christianity would not come till late in 1931, when he finally came to understand the nature and origin of myth. From his years as a teen until his conversion, Lewis, while loving the power of myth, all but abandoned (along with his Christianity) any connections it might have to reality or truth—until an important conversation with his friends J. R. R. Tolkien and Hugo Dyson. On September 19, 1931, Lewis had Dyson and Tolkien to dinner. The conversation lasted till 3:00 A.M. with Tolkien (and another hour with just Lewis and Dyson). Humphrey Carpenter's explanation of the conversation (from Tolkien's perspective) emphasizes the influence of Tolkien's view of myth and language. Carpenter explains that Lewis had come to believe in God, but not Christianity. He could not understand the purpose of the Crucifixion and the Resurrection. Why were they necessary? Without understanding the "function of Christ in Christianity," he could not believe.[20]

Tolkien and Dyson responded by arguing that Lewis was making a demand on Christianity that he didn't need to make. Whenever Lewis encountered the sacrifice or death of a god in pagan religion, he found it moving. The dying and reviving god that Lewis encountered in the stories of Adonis, Osiris, and, especially, Balder were a delight to his imagination. Why, then, couldn't Lewis experience this same mythic delight when he encountered the dying and reviving God in the Gospels? Lewis's answer was that the myths weren't making any truth claims, and Christianity was. As Carpenter has him put it, "myths are lies, even though lies breathed through silver."[21] And to this, Tolkien replied, "No, they are not." Carpenter suggests Tolkien's argument went something like this:

You call a tree a tree, he said, and you think nothing more of the word. But it was not a "tree" until someone gave it that name. You call a star a star, and say it is just a ball of matter moving on a mathematical course. But that is merely how *you* see it. By so naming things and describing them you are only inventing your own terms about them. And just as speech is invention about objects and ideas, so myth is invention about truth.[22]

Lewis's own explanation of the event does not contradict this account, but shifts the emphasis to the relationship between myth and fact, emphasizing Christianity and its mythic qualities. When Lewis could finally see Christianity as being myth as well as fact—that is, when Lewis's own demand for mythic wonder on the one side and rational reality on the other finally met in Christianity—he was able to believe. In a letter of September 22 to Arthur Greeves, Lewis mentions the conversation with Tolkien and Dyson, saying they began with myth and metaphor.[23] Then, in a letter of October 1, Lewis tells Greeves that he has come to believe not only in God but in Christ,[24] and he credits the conversation with Dyson and Tolkien.

Lewis explains the conversation in detail in his next letter to Greeves, saying that he had been held back for a year, not so much by an inability to believe but by an inability to understand why the death of Christ mattered. He said, "you can't believe a thing while you are ignorant *what* the thing is."[25] Lewis could not understand how the death of Christ two thousand years ago could open up heaven to everyone in the world. Dyson and Tolkien showed him that, though he was moved by stories of the "god sacrificing himself to himself" and the "dying and reviving god" in pagan myths (including Adonis, Osiris, and Balder), he was not so moved by the same story in the Gospels.[26] "The reason was that in Pagan stories I was prepared to feel the myth as profound and suggestive of meanings beyond my grasp even tho' I could not say in cold prose 'what it meant.'" He then came to the new understanding that the story of Jesus Christ is a "true myth," one that affects us like any other myth—but with this one key difference: "it really happened." But what matters is that we have to accept the story with the same pleasure and wonder that we receive any myth,

> remembering that it is God's myth where the others are men's myths: i.e., the Pagan stories are God expressing Himself through the minds of poets, using such images as He found there while Christianity is God expressing Himself through what we call "real things." Therefore it is *true,* not in the sense of being a "description" of God (that no finite mind could take in) but in the sense of being the way in which God chooses to (or can) appear to our faculties. The "doctrines" we get *out of* the true myth are of course *less* true; already expressed in a language more adequate, namely the actual incarnation, crucifixion, and resurrection.[27]

In pagan stories, God is expressing His mind through the pagan poets (remember the idea of the origin of myth we encountered in *Perelandra:* an environment of minds—a web in which all minds, even in the fallen world are yet tangled[28]). In Christianity, God expresses Himself in a myth that actually happened in history.

What Lewis as a Christian thus came to believe about myth is, perhaps, best expressed in his essay, "Religion without Dogma?" where he begins with various traditional views on the nature of myth that has been seen as

> literally true . . . , allegorically true . . . , as confused history . . . , as priestly lies . . . , as imitative agricultural ritual mistaken for propositions. . . . If you start from a naturalistic philosophy, then something like the view of Euhemerus [confused history] or . . . Frazer [agricultural ritual] is likely to result. But I am not a naturalist. I believe that in the huge mass of mythology which has come down to us a good many different sources are mixed—true history, allegory, ritual, the human delight in

> story telling. . . . But among these sources I include the su-
> pernatural, both diabolical and divine. We need here concern
> ourselves only with the latter. If my religion is erroneous then
> occurrences of similar motifs in pagan stories are . . . instances
> of the same . . . error. But if my religion is true, then these
> stories may well be a *preparatio evangelica,* a divine hinting in
> poetic and ritual form at the same central truth which was
> later focused and . . . historicised in the Incarnation.[29]

Lewis concludes that he would not have become a Christian if it meant saying that other religions in the world were completely wrong. Indeed, his conversion came because he saw Christianity as the fulfillment of something that had always been, at least to some degree, a part of human understanding.[30]

Lewis attributes myth to a variety of sources: history, allegory, ritual, storytelling, and supernatural sources, both divine and diabolical. Lewis also relates what he believes to be God's major purpose for myth in the world.[31] God has sent myth—as "splinters of truth"—into the world as a revelation. Specifically, divine myth serves as a *preparatio evangelica,* a means of preparing humanity for the coming of the Gospel, the myth that became fact. All the sacrificial gods of all the greater myths were the "first shadowy approach of something whose reality came with Christ."[32]

In *Perelandra* we saw that myth is "gleams of celestial strength and beauty falling on a jungle of filth and imbecility."[33] In *Miracles* Lewis defines myth as a "real though unfocused gleam of divine truth falling on human imagination."[34] These definitions fit the idea that myth's origins include human corruption, demonic influence, but also divine influence.

Lewis also suggests an alternative possibility for the sources of myth: that the events in some myths might have really happened. Of course, Lewis *did* believe it happened with Christ. But he sometimes wondered if it happened with other myths as well. We saw this possibility in the poem "A Footnote to Pre-history," in which Adam and Eve encounter mythic creatures after the Fall—creatures wiped away by Noah's flood, but whose memory is passed on through the collective unconscious.[35] We also saw Lewis hint at this possibility in *Perelandra,* when Ransom wonders about a past long gone in which satyrs really did dance in the Italian countryside.[36]

An alternate approach to myth as reality was once suggested to Lewis by Tolkien who said that the way people felt about "home" must have been something very different in times past, when families ate the food they farmed themselves on the same scant miles of ground for generation after generation. Perhaps such people saw nymphs in the water and dryads among the trees because there was in some way a real, not merely meta-phorical, connection between the people and the land on which they lived. Earth and air, corn and bread—these things of the land were somehow really inside the folk who lived there.[37]

We haven't looked at everything C. S. Lewis had to say about myth. But we have enough now to understand the remaining books in Tumnus's library, pushing further exploration on Lewis's theory of myth to a later chapter.

CHAPTER EIGHT

Men, Monks, and Gamekeepers; a Study in Popular Legend

I pointed out in the introduction to part III that the words *legend* and *myth* as used in the titles of the second two books on Tumnus's bookshelf have negative connotations—the legends and myths seem not so likely to be true. However, what *is* likely is that the "study" going on in *Men, Monks, and Gamekeepers; a Study in Popular Legend* suggests Tumnus's hope that such wondrous creatures might yet be found in Narnia. Just as Lewis wondered if satyrs, giants, dwarfs, and unicorns once existed in our world, so might Tumnus (along with the authors of the books on his shelves) wonder about the existence of men in his world.

Men

We learn from later Narnian books that the "men" referenced in this book's title once did exist in Narnia. *The Magician's Nephew* tells us that the first kings and queens of Narnia were human, and humans were even present at the creation of Narnia.[1] But the Narnian reality in *The Lion, the Witch and the Wardrobe* is that men are only popular legend; there aren't any human beings to be found there. Although Lewis likely did not fully envision the history and origin story of Narnia while writing the first book in the series, we might speculate that the White Witch's hundred-year winter, and whatever steps she took in the past to take control of Narnia, wiped the memory of men from native Narnians (save for a few legendary tales) and isolated Narnia from all outside influences. However it happened, the references to men in the books on Tumnus's shelf suggest a fundamental question about whether or not sons of Adam and daughters of Eve exist—or ever existed. My guess is that the Narnians would very much like them to.

Gamekeepers

The importance of the "gamekeepers" referenced in the title is explained easily enough. In a land of talking animals, there are no gamekeepers. The Narnian animals neither need nor would put up with a bunch of paid human dogcatchers—or fauncatchers or nymph-catchers—penning them up and telling them where they can and can't roam. They're already unhappy with the witch for doing exactly that.

We should remember that there are nonspeaking animals in other Narnian books. In fact Shasta and Bree come under the cruel hands of some Calormene gamekeepers who don't know they're talking horses, and our Narnian equines do their best to escape them. But we can reply, again, that *The Lion, the Witch and the Wardrobe*, being the first book in the series, was written by a Lewis who might not yet have added lower animals to his world. In Narnia, gamekeepers are pure legend, probably *not* the kind Narnians would like to see come into reality, a point that reminds us of a cautionary lesson.

Throughout this book, I've made it clear that Lewis valued myth for its ability to connect us to a reality that is truer than the one we see around us. I'll develop this view of myth and its connection to knowledge even further in chapter 10—but we can't dismiss the lesson raised by the gamekeepers in Tumnus's book. Myths contain prismatic rays of divine light, but those slight beams are falling on a world of grime and stupidity. Myths include divine influence, but they also include the lies of priests and demonic influence. Perhaps these influences come in varying levels. Perhaps some myths contain no connection to truth at all, while others contain much. Or perhaps myths that do contain some truth are utterly misread and misused—as Lewis notes of the Nazis' misuse and utter misunderstanding of Norse mythology in his essay "First and Second Things." Lewis calls the Nazi attempt to appropriate the Nordic myth absurd, asking what business the Nazis have, when they believe might makes right, to claim they worship Odin. Of all ancient mythologies, Norse religion was the one that instructed people to serve and worship gods who were up against a wall and would ultimately lose the war they were fighting.[2]

As to Narnians, they want nothing to do with gamekeepers in the same way that you and I would prefer myths in which a god dies and is reborn to save his people rather than myths that call for regular human sacrifice.

Monks

Well, that leaves the "monks" referenced in this book's title. What are we supposed to do with them? Why focus on these priestly fellows? Just as dryads and centaurs appear as myth in our world but are real in Narnia, so monks are real in our world but are Narnian myth. But why the emphasis on them? Why not something like "airplanes" instead?

A simplistic answer would be to say the word makes for nice alliteration of *men* and *monks* in the title. Lewis loved poetic device and meter. Some of his poetry shows extreme complexity of rhyme and meter—something for which Lewis gets too little credit.[3] He loved the sounds of words. Walter Hooper once told me that when Lewis wrote, he would sound out the words in a low whisper. For Lewis, words were for the ear as well as the eye. Hooper said this was one of the reasons that Lewis didn't like writing with a fountain pen (and he hated the clanking of typewriter keys): he wanted the pause that occurred after writing six words or so—a pause during which he had to re-dip his pen—so that he could keep himself in sync with the rhythm of the words he was writing. But though we shouldn't underestimate Lewis's love for and use of sound device, he must have had more reason than alliteration for putting the word *monks* in this title.

This, in fact, was the word that most intrigued me in the titles of Tumnus's books. A year before I started to develop this topic for a conference speech, I had reviewed the titles in Tumnus's library and noticed for the first time this little word. This, along with the conference theme, "Is Man a Myth?" piqued my curiosity and led me to write this book. Ironically, solving the problem of the term *monks* was a very early part of the process. Here's what I think:

Obviously there aren't any monks in Narnia; they are a legend—that's the starting point. That part's easy. But then why aren't there any animal equivalents? Why aren't there any Narnian priests? While there's plenty of talk of prophecies and Aslan and his father, the great Emperor-beyond-the-Sea, there is no organized (or even disorganized) religion in Narnia. No Protestymphs, no Badgertists, no Satyrthodox, no Motherhen Church. I don't believe Lewis is advocating the abandonment of organized religion. But apparently the animals of Narnia just don't need it. They have Aslan. He may have been gone for the last hundred years, but it's not too much of an attack on their faith (though it proves so for some Narnians after a longer period of his absence in *Prince Caspian*).[4] Even in the secular age of *Prince Caspian*, most of the creatures of Narnia remain faithful to Aslan, especially the badgers, who have long memories.[5] Something of this sentiment is expressed by Lewis in his essay "Revival or Decay." In the defense of formal religion, he notes that religious people aren't interested in religion but in God. The maenads didn't think about religion; they thought about Dionysus.[6]

So monks are myths in Narnia. But notice that they are "popular" legends. Why? Well, again, it shows that Lewis was not intending to be negative toward monks or organized religion. Instead, just as sylvans are the embodiment of nature as Lewis conceives it—that is, nature as a living, spiritual organism endowed with meaning by God, as opposed to nature as a mindless machine—so are monks the mythic, living embodiment of the religious impulse, the impulse to pursue God. And this would be utterly significant to those Narnians who still very much want to pursue Aslan. The appearance of a monk in Narnia would be no less welcome, no less spiritually important than the appearance of Silenus, Bacchus, or four children who might fulfill the prophecy of Cair Paravel. What is fact in our world—that there are human beings who dedicate their lives to the pursuit of God in an organized, traditional, even ritualistic way—is wondrous myth to the creatures of Narnia. The whole thing suggests the kind of wonder that Caspian feels when he learns that our Earth is actually round! He would very much like to see a land that's shaped into a sphere.[7]

The Mythic Approach to Reading

Something similar occurs in *The Lord of the Rings*. While we look at Middle-earth as a fairy-tale land filled with magic, the denizens of Middle-earth themselves do not see it that way. For them it's all rather ordinary; encounters with magic are not so frequent. Elrond's eyewitness accounts of the Second Age of Middle-earth are a wonder to Frodo,[8] and the men of Rohan and Gondor find Lothlorien to be a frighteningly mythic place.[9] Theoden expresses surprise at first meeting Merry and Pippin, since in his experience hobbits are the stuff of legend.[10]

If within the mythic worlds of Middle-earth and Narnia the people perceive certain things mythically, we ought to do the same with Narnia in our own world by making a choice about how we read the books—that is, by choosing to read them mythically. To explain what I mean, I want us to turn to another key idea in Lewis's theory of myth. While having many profound meanings, while being connected to truth and reality in significant ways, myth for Lewis is also a type of story. Lewis defines myth as a category or genre of literature: "A *Myth* is the description of a state, an event, or a series of events, involving superhuman personages, possessing unity, not truly implying a particular time or place, and dependent for its contents not on motives developed in the course of action but on the immutable relations of the personages."[11] Lewis explains elements of this definition in a more thorough literary discussion of myth in *An Experiment in Criticism,* where he defines myth by describing its effects on a reader (or receiver—he believes myth can come to us through methods other than literature as well). Lewis identifies six characteristics of our experience of myth as story:

1. Myth is "extra-literary."[12] Lewis explains that a mythic story is important apart from "its embodiment in any literary work."[13] The myth is not to be found in the language that conveys it, but in the elements of the story itself: the events of the plot, the setting, the kinds of creatures and types of characters that appear in it.

2. What pleasure we get from myth does not come from "such usual narrative attractions as suspense or surprise." The events of the story come across to us with a sense of inevitability or familiarity. To encounter a myth is to meet a "permanent object of contemplation—more like a thing than a narration."[14]

3. In myth we do not identify with the characters. "They are like shapes moving in another world. We feel indeed that the pattern of their movements has a profound relevance to our own life, but we do not imaginatively transport ourselves into theirs."

4. Myths are always "fantastic." They deal "with impossibles and preter-naturals."

5. Experiencing a myth "may be sad or joyful but it is always grave."

6. And the experience of a myth is not just grave, it inspires awe. "We feel it to be numinous . . . as if something of great moment had been communicated to us." And when the mind recurrently returns to the myth in order to grasp or analyze it, the *something* that the mind is trying to grasp can never quite be attained—this is apparent in our tendency to explain myths through allegory. But after all the allegories have been attempted, there's still something in the myth itself that feels more important.

In encountering a myth, we encounter something larger than ourselves, something larger than even an author's intentions for the mythic tale he is telling. What we encounter can be reduced—but cannot be *merely* reduced—to allegorized abstractions.

Lewis understood a difference between myth and allegory very early in his thinking. While working on his narrative poem *Dymer,* he considered it important to "keep the MYTH true and intrude as little invention of conscious allegory as might be."[15] The word *conscious* here is key. Lewis describes the major difference between myth and allegory as having to do with conscious intention and multiplicity of meanings. He claims "that a good myth (i.e., a story out of which ever varying meanings will grow for different readers and in different ages) is a higher thing than an allegory (into which *one* meaning has been put). Into an allegory a man can put only what he already knows: in a myth he puts what he does not yet know and c[oul]d not come to know in any other way."[16] Allegory is conscious, and its meanings are specific. In allegory, correlation between sign and signified is consciously, deliberately applied; the sign has only one meaning and that is predetermined by the author. In myth, on the other hand, meanings are multiple, fluid, and greater than the author's conscious intent.[17] I might go so far as to say the difference between allegory and myth is that allegory contains meaning, but myth simply *means*.[18]

One of the practical applications to be made from this look at how myth affects us as readers is in regard to a simple, but for some reason controversial Narnian question: in what order should we read the Chronicles of Narnia? The typical argument is between chronological order and the order of original publication. In the former, *The Magician's Nephew* is chronogically first. In the latter, it's published sixth. Briefly, I want to suggest that reading *The Magician's Nephew* later is the better option as it provides a more mythical experience when we read the whole series. If we read the origin story of Narnia first, we read it as a fantasy tale. It certainly is mythic to us. But myth is about the vast interplay of meanings a text has to offer. In a myth, the story is thick with connections, meanings, hints, and possibilities. When I read *The Magician's Nephew* first, I am intrigued by the lamppost, even delighted by it. But when I read the book in publication order, the lamppost, the tree that becomes the wardrobe, the witch, and Aslan himself all take on additional mythic meaning. My response is mythic wonder, doubled delight, because I am already familiar with these images. I add meanings to the already existing meanings I have of them. *The Magician's Nephew* read sixth and last becomes for me not just a fairy tale of Narnia, but the myth of Narnia's creation. When a first-time reader of the Narnia Chronicles reads *The Magician's Nephew* first, he reads it as a Terran who is encountering Narnia for the first time. When he reads it sixth, he reads it as a Narnian—or at least a human who has experienced Narnia—and its entire origin story takes on a mythic gravity that can't be experienced in reading it first. In short, for the Narnians, the tale of *The Magician's Nephew* isn't just a historical story. It's their origin myth. If we want to experience it the same way they do, we have to read it *after* we've been in Narnia for a while.

CHAPTER NINE

Is Man a Myth?

In *The Lion, the Witch and the Wardrobe,* men are mythic creatures; Lewis probably hadn't placed them in Archenland or Calormen yet (and if he had, we can suppose that the White Witch isolated all of Narnia from outside human influence). In *Prince Caspian,* good men (the kings and queens of old) are a myth—Trumpkin doesn't believe in them.[1] And, of course, the Telmarines don't believe in any of the Narnian creatures.

In *The Silver Chair,* the Green Lady tries to convince the Narnians that their entire world is a lie.[2] Her statements parallel the demythologizing activity of Sigmund Freud's claim that religion is just wish fulfillment, a notion that Lewis destroys in *The Pilgrim's Regress* by pointing out that Freud's rejection of God can also be labeled an example of wish fulfillment.[3] In fact, Lewis would argue that Freud was merely replacing an old myth with a new one, a myth of progress through materialistic evolution to replace the myths of religion. In his essay "The Funeral of a Great Myth," Lewis charts the development of the evolutionary myth from its pre-Darwinian roots in philosophy and literature through its death as a myth of the greatness of human progress.[4]

In trying to explain this demythologizing trend, though, I like to point out that science fiction is a genre that arose to replace fairy tales, but its roots are in the same desire for the wondrous and fantastic that humanity has always had. The myth of scientific materialism took our love for fairies on the fictional side and angels on the theological side and turned it into a love for aliens. For a really good example of this demythologizing activity, which is really only the substitution of a myth of naturalism for a myth of supernaturalism, take a look at Michael Crichton's book *Eaters of the Dead* (which was made into the film, *The 13th Warrior*). Crichton took everything science believed it knew about primitive European culture and applied it to the Beowulf saga. *Eaters of the Dead* is Beowulf without the supernatural elements. Crichton might have said his book was Beowulf demythologized. Lewis would have said it was Crichton substituting one myth for another.

Is man a myth? The question is full of potential meanings. The first of these is the one plainest to the context of *The Lion, the Witch and the Wardrobe:* the Narnians don't know if humans exist, but they very much hope they do. In this sense, the question could be considered from the common perspective that myth is "untrue." The Narnians would answer about man in the same way that we would answer about Chimera or the Minotaur. The second is the meaning applied in Lewis's "The Empty Universe," and it directly involves the demythologizing of mankind by naturalism. In this sense, the question could be considered from the modern perspective that subverts a unified concept of "man." In the essay, Lewis traces the long process by which Western thought de-anthropomorphized nature and, not stopping there, de-anthropomorphized humanity itself. Some of us will recall a book written in the 1970s by B. F. Skinner called *Beyond Freedom and Dignity,* which I believe was so titled in response to something Lewis had said in *The Abolition of Man.* Skinner's famous behaviorist psychology, which reduced man to mere behaviors and behavioral responses, has since been debunked by new discoveries in cognitive psychology and neural science, discoveries that suggest at least the possibility that there's more than a brain going on inside this head—there's also a mind. I say that, but then work in artificial intelligence, when it's applied to philosophy (by scientists who end up being bad philosophers), raises the brain/mind question again, moving us back to man the sentimental myth.

Regardless, if we ask C. S. Lewis whether or not man is a myth after the fashion of modern philosophy and the more common, negative definition of myth (i.e., myth as untruth), Lewis would reply that we are *not* a myth. We are real; we are human beings endowed with souls; we are not overly sophisticated animals; we are not mere social constructs inhabiting the lies our culture has devised about us.

In fact, Lewis might go even further and offer a significant third meaning to the question—one that considers it with a positive view of myth in mind. Myth is a way of glimpsing glory, of discovering God. In this sense, Lewis would argue that man is not a myth, and that is exactly the problem!

If myth does anything for us, it shows us glory—it fills us with wonder. It does this in two ways. First, myth "takes all the things we know and restores to them the rich significance which has been hidden by 'the veil of familiarity.'" Consider the example of a child sitting down to a lunch of cold meat. He finds that he can enjoy an otherwise dull meal by imagining himself having just shot a buffalo on the vast American plain with his own bow and now sitting down to feast on the fresh kill. The real meat before him becomes more delicious because it has been "dipped in a story." A landscape in a mirror is more magical. And when we put the stuff of life, "bread, gold, horse, apple, or the very roads into a myth," we do not escape from reality but discover it anew. While the story remains with us, the real things of life are somehow more real, more what they were meant to be. "By dipping them in myth we see them more clearly."[5] Myth, you see, shows us glory in the stuff of life—the very world we live in—by lifting the veil of the familiar from our imaginations.

The second way myth shows us glory is even more direct. In *The Great Divorce,* a ghostly painter has entered the outskirts of heaven and is having a conversation with a heavenly resident who was his friend on earth. While talking about art, this friend reminds the painter that he painted on earth because he had glimpsed the heavenly landscape through the earthly one, and the reason his paintings were successful was that they gave others the power to glimpse the heavenly beauty as well.[6]

These two methods for revealing glory through myth are suggested to us in the afterword to *The Pilgrim's Regress.* Here, and in *Surprised by Joy,* Lewis relates how his search for God had two prongs or modes of progress: in reason and in imagination. Lewis the philosopher came to a belief in God largely due to his understanding that the act of reasoning would be invalid if there were no higher power of reason that makes it so. If the mind does not exist, then thoughts in the brain cannot be trusted as accurate. But then there was the lover of beauty in nature, of poetry, and of myth. The imaginative Lewis was drawn into aesthetic experience, an experience he defined as an intense longing for some unnamed thing, a longing that felt so good that having that desire was better than having any other kind of fulfillment. He first encountered this experience, which he labeled "joy," in a model of a garden his brother had made when Lewis was a child. After that, Lewis would experience it in the beauty of nature and in literature, especially fantastic literature—fairy tales, myth, and most poignantly in Norse myth. At first Lewis believed each of these things to be the object he was longing for. For a while he also thought this object might be romantic love and the sexual satisfaction that goes with it. Eventually he came to realize none of these things would fulfill his longing. The inexpressible, unattainable thing he wanted was so utterly "other" that he came to realize it must be God.[7]

Lewis concluded in *Mere Christianity* that "If I find in myself a desire which no experience in this world can satisfy, the most probable explanation is that I was made for another world."[8] The key idea, here, is that Lewis looks at myth as a source of longing. This is, I think, because he sees myth as a source for glimpses of the heavenly landscape—the heavenly glory—on earth. I might almost say that myth for Lewis is events or facts as they would have occurred in a world where their glory had not been stripped from them. Consider the relationship between myth, fact, and glory as described in *Miracles:* "Just as God, in becoming Man, is 'emptied' of His glory, so the truth, when it comes down from the 'heaven' of myth to the 'earth' of history, undergoes a certain humiliation. Hence [scripture] is, and ought to be, more prosaic, in some ways less *splendid*, . . . less rich in many kinds of imaginative beauty than the Pagan mythologies."[9] Clearly, for Lewis, myth gives us glimpses of heavenly glory.

In "The Weight of Glory," Lewis takes his experience of longing and applies it to the biblical concept of glory. He speaks first about the longing we all feel: a desire for a "far-off country" that we refuse to admit we long for. A desire so secret that we take revenge on it by passing it off as nostalgia or labeling it "romanticism" or attributing it to the foolishness of youth. Stranger still is the paradox that "it is a desire for something that has never actually appeared in our experience [but] our experience is constantly suggesting it. . . . Our commonest expedient is to call it beauty and behave as if that had settled the matter."[10]

Next, Lewis considers the promises of heaven, chiefly the fact that we will enter into God's glory. He notes the strangeness of this promise since "glory" seems to reference fame—a not-so-Christian virtue—and, well, bright light.[11] He explains the former in terms of God's eternal recognition. Earthly fame is vain because it fades. The glory of heaven is the glory of being acknowledged by the eternal, infinite recognition of God. It is to be told (as in Christ's parable) "well done, good and faithful servant" once and for all, unto eternity.[12] The glory we associate with appearance—especially the appearance of light—Lewis connects to beauty, and this takes us back to his concept of longing or desire that produces joy—the joy we experience when we encounter beauty. This is a thing we long for; this is a thing we desire: to experience a beauty *in* the world that comes from *beyond* the world. But, as Lewis notes, even that is not enough.

In an earlier chapter, I quoted "The Weight of Glory" where Lewis writes of our not wanting to merely behold beauty, but of our wanting to be joined with that beauty. I want to continue that quote: "That is why we have peopled air and earth and water with gods and goddesses and nymphs and elves—that, though we cannot, yet these projections can enjoy in themselves that beauty, grace, and power of which Nature is the image."[13] Do you see what Lewis is saying? We people the earth with mythic creatures because they represent the beauty, grace, and power for which we desperately long—a glory, a light behind all lights, which nevertheless shines through in perceptible light and beauty. Nature is an image of that glory for which we long, especially to have in ourselves—it's not enough to see beauty: we want to be beautiful; we want the promised glory in us. These myths of magical creatures are prophetic of what is yet to come for us: "an eternal weight of glory," as Paul says, "far beyond all comparison."[14]

But we don't have it yet: we are not even fully human—we don't even have the glory meant for us on earth (let alone in heaven). Do you remember Ransom's response, at the end of *Perelandra,* when he sees the king and queen, the Adam and Eve of Venus in their glory for the first time? He falls at their feet, barely able to gaze upon them, and speaks in a broken voice: "I have never before seen a man or a woman. I have lived all my life among shadows and broken images."[15] But here before Ransom are *royal* parents, the likes of which he's never seen on Earth. We are waiting for a glory we don't yet have, a glory that will make us into myths, into gods. That may seem a strange statement, even blasphemous. But in John 10:34, Jesus says, "Has it not been written in your Law, 'I said, you are gods'?"[16] He then says that it is God who has said we are gods (the Hebrew word is *elohim*). It's a quirky passage on which I have never heard a single sermon. Lewis echoes the sentiment in "The Empty Universe" essay, reminding us we once saw *ourselves* as "akin to the gods." Perhaps we get no sermons on the John passage here because this wondrous claim about human beings, a quote from Psalm 82:6, is followed in that psalm by the most terrible of truths. It reads: "I said, 'You are gods, and all of you are sons of the Most High. Nevertheless you will die like men. . . .'"[17]

We were meant to be myths, but the mythic world has withdrawn from us. We were meant to be gods of the earth, and we are not. Lewis concludes his sad poem "Passing To-day by a Cottage, I Shed Tears" by saying, "Gods we are, Thou has said: and we pay dearly."[18] In context, the poem is saying we pay dearly for our sufferings on earth, but we also pay because we have lost our glory-filled status. We are myth-less, glory-less, subhuman creatures. If we *were* myth, everyone would know it; the attempts we make at turning man into something less than what he is would stop: We wouldn't be advanced apes. Minds wouldn't be just complex brains. Gender wouldn't be a mere description of sex organs, but a spiritual reality. Human beings from conception to old age and death—though, of course, there wouldn't be any death—would be the most valuable resources on the planet.

We get a glimpse of him every now and then, you know—mythic man: In a hero who makes a woman's heart flutter (despite our best attempts to tell women they don't need the son of a king—a prince—to come and rescue them). In a woman so beautiful that men have to look away because it hurts too much to go on gazing (or out of shame because they've been taught to either turn her beauty into objectifying lust or ignore her beauty because it's said to equal objectifying lust).

If someone told me I could live on this earth forever, that they'd discovered the cure for death, I'd tell them, "No thanks."

The promise of heaven is not merely a promise of eternal life; it's a promise of transformation through being filled with God's glory. That's what I want. I want to be a real man like I was meant to be. I want to know the mythic stature to which I've been called.

This explains an important Lewisian idea, that of the "intolerable compliment." God has paid us an intolerable compliment in that He will not settle for our being mediocre people living mediocre lives. This is because each human being is a divinely created work that God is always forming. As such, He will not be satisfied until the work has achieved perfection. An artist won't give much time or trouble over a sketch made in practice. But to his greatest masterpiece he will devote the greatest pains and care and so *give* the greatest care and pain as if the picture were alive and could perceive the master's work. Imagine a self-aware painting "after being rubbed and scraped and re-commenced for the tenth time, wishing that it were only a thumb-nail sketch whose making was over in a minute." We're like that; there are times when we'd gladly wish God had created us for a destiny that is less glorious and therefore less difficult.[19] "Gods we are, Thou has said: and we pay dearly."[20] Man is not a myth, and that is a serious, deeply spiritual problem. I hope this tragic status is one Aslan overcomes in us very soon.

Part IV

Beyond the Bookshelf

We've looked at the faun's bookshelf, but we haven't looked at everything C. S. Lewis said about myth. Tumnus's books don't take us down every path we need to follow. In this last part of our study, we will look at what Lewis believed about mythic thought, explore his love of Norse myth, and consider what may be a contradiction in Lewis's own thoughts about myth.

CHAPTER TEN

Mythic Knowing

That we are not myths is one way of saying we are fallen; to say that we need and long to be made into mythic beings is to say that we need redemption to glory. I'm left then with a question about myth as we encounter it in the fallen world: if we are not now mythic, can we yet think and perceive mythically and make use of such mythic knowledge? What we're about to explore contains the most complicated ideas Lewis and some of the other Inklings shared about myth. We're going to look at myth's connection to how human knowledge works. In philosophical terms, we're going to look at the relationship between myth and epistemology (the theory of knowing). It won't be easy, so grab a cup of tea, settle in, and think deep thoughts.

At the beginning of this book, I pointed to the power of myth by having us look at the fact that the two most popular stories of the twentieth century were myths: *The Lord of the Rings* and *Star Wars*. We've looked at some reasons why. I want to suggest one more: that myth represents a kind of thinking that may be closer to the thought processes of men and women in a perfect state. Mythic thinking belongs to Eden and heaven and may be the most important kind of thinking we're meant for. But it may also be a dangerous mode of thought—one deserving some caution.

Meaning, Imagination, and Truth

In order to understand mythic thought, we have to talk about more than just myth; we have to talk about meaning. "What does it mean?" is a question we ask all the time, often about the symbols and images we encounter in books, songs, and movies. But do we ever ask what *meaning* itself means? Usually when we ask for the meaning of a word, a line in a song, or a symbolic image, we want an explanation in words. My favorite example of this idea comes from a movie-watching experience. In *The Empire Strikes Back,* Luke journeys down into his own cave of knowledge and confronts Darth Vader. He cuts Vader's head clean off, only to find his own face looking back at him.[1] My daughter first watched this movie with me when she was around ten, and she asked me what this scene *meant.* I told her, "It means Luke's worst enemy is himself. He has to fight his own fear and doubt before he can face the real Darth Vader. What happened in the cave was a dream or vision." I explained the meaning in words. But movies mean more than the words in them. Their magic is in the meanings they communicate *beyond* words. Their truth is in their images and experiential quality.

In an essay called "Bluspels and Flalansferes," Lewis helps us search for the meaning of *meaning.* At the end of a long discussion on metaphor, meaning, and imagination, Lewis says that he is not trying to argue that the imagination is the "organ of truth." He hasn't been talking about truth, but about meaning, "which is the antecedent condition both of truth and falsehood." The opposite of meaning isn't falsehood, but "nonsense"; however, it's only by the meaning-making ability of imagination that either truth or falsehood are possible. Lewis concludes that "reason is the natural organ of truth; but imagination is the organ of meaning."[2] What Lewis argues here, among other things, is that meaning is not the same thing as truth—the one belongs to the faculty of imagination, the other to the faculty of reason.

The first important idea we get from this text, then, is about the connection between imagination and meaning.

The reason it's important is because Lewis associates myth with imagination. In *The Pilgrim's Regress,* he specifically writes that myth "must be grasped with the imagination, not with the intellect."[3] Elsewhere he says it is "imagination that makes myth."[4] Again, "the mythopoeic is . . . a mode of imagination which does something to us at a deep level."[5]

Myth and imagination are connected in Lewis's thinking, but they are not the same thing. Lewis's simplest definition of imagination occurs in *Miracles:* "We can imagine: that is, we can cause to exist the mental pictures of material objects, and even human characters, and events."[6] According to Peter Schakel, Lewis uses the term *imagination* in several ways:

> as the image-making power ("imagine two books lying on a ta-ble"), the creative or inventive power ("fired the imagination of the *hrossa*"), the power to make up things ("of course one can imagine things"), the power to create fiction ("solely an imagi-native supposal"), the mysteriousness and adventurousness of romance ("almost everything the imagination craves—irony, heroism, vastness, unity in multiplicity, and a tragic close"), and "'Imagination' in some high Coleridgean sense."[7]

In the last of these, imagination is seen as a key to perception, creativity, knowledge, and encounters with the transcendent—for Coleridge it had nothing less than spiritual significance. Lewis connected it to the sense of longing for the unnamed transcendent thing he spoke of in "The Weight of Glory"; he referred to that longing as "joy."[8]

While this last definition of imagination is significant, the most basic definitions may be more important to our initial un-derstanding of myth. In our imaginations, we are able to mimic experience; we can do this not only by repeating experiences (through memory), but by inventing whole new experiences. These can include experiences we've never been through ourselves as well as magical, fantastical experiences that no one has been through *except* in his or her imagination.

To encounter myth, then, is not to encounter truth or a series of truths so much as it is to encounter an experience or experiences. This doesn't mean there is no connection between myth and truth, as we'll see shortly, but it's very important we get right what the connection is. In "Bluspels and Flalansferes," the imagination provides meanings that make it possible for reason to find truths. But as we add experience into the mix of understanding, especially the experience of myth, things get more complicated.

In chapter 8 we briefly looked at a limitation on myth. Though Lewis finds myth to contain kernels of truth—gleams of divine inspiration—he also acknowledges, however briefly, that among the myth-making influences in our world are demonic ones. Another potential problem with myth is that we encounter it in the imagination. In a rare warning about myth, Lewis writes that myth is made by imagination, and imagination only uses elements from rational thought that it "finds convenient."[9] In "Bluspels and Flalansferes," Lewis calls imagination the organ of meaning and reason the organ of truth, noting that without meanings there can be neither truths nor falsehoods. We have to contend with the epistemological implication of this idea, something Lewis scholars writing about myth and imagination (including myself) haven't sufficiently addressed until recently.[10] While Lewis's theory of myth suggests the relationship between imagination and truth is important, he nevertheless sees this limitation: that the imagination can be used for relating meanings that are false as well as true. In short, the imagination can be used as a vehicle to propagate lies.

Lewis points this out in several letters and works. He tells us the imagination is something that needs to be controlled (in the context of avoiding the temptation to brood over fears or grievances)[11] and that fear can be produced by the "illusions of the imagination."[12] He warns that changing the church's liturgy—its imaginative forms—may result in a liturgy that creates in people through "suggestion" a belief that the church doesn't actually profess as part of its doctrine.[13] And Lewis specifically writes that it's possible for us to commit sins with the imagination,[14] especially in regard to sexual sin, noting additionally that "sensuality really arises more from the imagination" than it does from bodily desires.[15]

The imagination can also be used to launch attacks against our faith. Dorothy Sayers defines faith as "imagination actualized by will"[16]—something along the lines, I think, of seeing with a God's-eye point of view. Lewis would perhaps agree; however, he notes that our faith falters less when it is presented with logical counterarguments than when faith itself appears (to the imagination and the emotions) to be improbable. Take the example of learning to swim. If the lifeguard teaching you to swim tells you you're safe, you may believe him or you may not. Odds are, if you don't believe him, you won't be able to cite any good reasons for not doing so. Lewis says it's not reason that keeps you from believing in this instance, it's your experience—your senses—and your imagination that will attack your belief. It's just as described in the New Testament: the battle is not faith versus reason, but faith versus sight.[17] Or take the example of going in for an operation. Those of us who have done so may have been plagued by a fear that the anesthesia won't work. Faced with such a situation—despite numerous doctors' assurances to the contrary—Lewis writes that he loses any faith he has in anesthetics. At that point, his faith isn't being taken away by reason, but by his emotions and his imagination; reason bolsters his faith, and so the battle he endures is one in which reason and faith on one hand stand over against the senses and imagination on the other.[18]

Again, this is not to say the imagination has no value as a way of knowing. It's just that it has a double role. Lewis believes that everything, in its own way, can "reflect heavenly truth," including the imagination. Here, *reflect* is the key word. The "lower life of the imagination is not a beginning of, nor a step toward, the higher life of the spirit"; it is only an image (though God could transform it into "such a beginning").[19] In a frank letter on imagination and lust, Lewis writes that imagination has several true purposes, which include helping us to understand people other than ourselves and enjoying (and, for some, making) art; however, imagination also has an improper function, which is to "provide for us, in shadowy form, a substitute for virtues, successes, distinctions etc. which ought to be sought *outside* in the real world"—for example, imagining what we'd do with all our money if we were rich, rather than actually trying to make and save money.[20]

Because the imagination has both good and bad uses, Lewis thinks it utterly important that our imagination be guarded from attack and trained to pursue its good uses. Screwtape more than once argues the effectiveness of attacking imagination. In order to convince people that demons don't exist, he calls for the "textbook" practice of suggesting an image of "something in red tights," noting the fact that in "modern imagination" devils are "*comic* figures," which, with the right picture in a human's head, are very easy to dismiss as unbelievable.[21] Through imagination, Screwtape very specifically says myth can be used to propagate lies. In the seventh letter, he explains the devilish strategy of creating the "Materialist Magician" through convincing human beings to "emotionalise and mythologise their science" to the point that they start believing in demons without really knowing it.[22] In his opening letter, Screwtape chides Wormwood for attempting to use reason to dissuade his patient of the truth: "Jargon, not argument, is your best ally in keeping him from the Church," he claims, telling Wormwood not to bother with trying to prove to the man that materialism is the truth. Instead, he should make him feel that it's "strong, or stark, or courageous."[23] The appeal is to imaginative metaphor, not to propositional truth. The Un-man in *Perelandra* makes a similar attack on the Queen—the Eve of Venus—in trying to get her to defy God's one law for her there. Though he begins with reasoned arguments, the demon-possessed man eventually turns to appealing to her vanity and to her imaginative sense of the heroic, the latter by telling her stories of great women from Earth who defied the law and were proclaimed right for doing so, despite their great suffering for it. Ransom comes to realize that, though the Queen's will has withstood the temptation, her imagination is becoming corrupted, and he must stop the Un-man from continuing to tempt her.[24] Because of possible demonic influence, Lewis also warns against attaching too much importance to visions. Though they may be what they seem, they may also be the "work of one's own imagination" or even "delusions sent by the enemy."[25]

For Lewis, training the imagination against evil becomes a matter of educational priority. In his fiction he gives us the example of Eustace Clarence Scrubb, a boy who has gone all wrong, in part because his imagination has been dulled by reading the wrong things—books that have much to say about economics, politics, and plumbing, but which are "weak on dragons"[26] and other wonders of the imagination.

In his nonfiction, Lewis makes the very serious point that children need to be taught right, or "just," sentiments. In the context of teaching literature, Lewis in *The Abolition of Man* defines the problem with failing to train people's imaginations about the genuine *value* to be found in the things of life. Plato and Aristotle said the purpose of education was to instill in children a sense of what they should and shouldn't like. Then, when they are old enough for reasoned thought, students who have been trained in these "'ordinate affections' or 'just sentiments' will easily find the first principles in Ethics"—that is, they will intuitively see right from wrong, which is forever invisible to the corrupted heart. Children have to be "trained to feel pleasure, liking, disgust, and hatred at those things which really are pleasant, likeable, disgusting, and hateful," and this must happen before they are old enough to reason, so that when reason finally comes to them they will receive it with open arms, recognizing the affinity they already share with it.[27] In failing to train the imagination in "just sentiments," we do so at our own cultural peril. One reason for this is clear: the imagination is an important faculty in human knowing, but it is one that can be filled with both truth and falsehood.

Even in regard to the use of imagination in pursuit of the creative impulse, Lewis notes a negative as well as a positive *kind* of imagination. In *An Experiment in Criticism,* as well as in his essay "Psycho-Analysis and Literary Criticism," Lewis distinguishes between "egoistic" and "disinterested" imagination.[28] The former exists solely to gratify the desires of the person doing the imagining.[29] The latter is a "free" activity of imagination because it is not constrained by the selfish impulse to escapism or castle building.[30] In the egoistic imagination, we make ourselves the center of attention—we imagine ourselves as the hero of the story we're creating. In the disinterested imagination, we invent for the good pleasure of invention; we get our own egos out of the way.

In his recent book, *Faith, Hope and Poetry,*[31] Malcolm Guite offers a much-needed study on the abandonment of imagination as a source of knowledge (especially in the form of poetry) in Western culture. The call to return to imaginative understanding is significant. I think the mistakes that result from abandoning an epistemology of imagination are especially clear in education (most of all in the teaching of ethics), the bankruptcy of modern trends in art, and the imposition of artificial methods of assessment and business-model approaches on educational institutions.

In other areas of culture, conversely, we should be looking to see how the unchecked imagination is causing *harm*. While the postmodern emphasis on narrative shows a resurgent concern for imagination as a mode of knowing, the postmodern rejection of any master narrative leaves our culture to create its own stories for making sense of our world. In other words, today people are inventing their own myths to explain the world or adopting popular new myths fed to them by various outlets of the mass media. The myth of *Star Wars* has produced a literal religious following. The pagan gods of the past have been replaced by the brightly costumed superheroes of comics and film (although Thor has managed to bridge the gap between both eras). Organized religion, which Christians would argue means real revelation from God handed down to man through scripture, the church, and the Incarnation of Christ—the myth that became fact—is being replaced by homegrown myths, even myths recognized as mythology (as pure fiction). Finding the balance between reason and imagination, between abandoning imagination as being truth-less, on the one hand, and using the imagination to reject truth, on the other, is the challenge of our current cultural situation.

In short, if the imagination can be fooled, and if myths come to us through the imagination, then clearly there are some limits to the knowledge myth can bring us. That said, Lewis never returns to the belief that myths are merely beautiful lies. They have a complex relationship with truth and the real—one worth putting in some effort to understand, a relationship in which imagination provides us an avenue to truths that can't be approached in any way *except* by imagination.

One way Lewis deals with the complicated connection between myth and truth is in discussing the relationship between poetry and theology. He was once asked to speak on a question that later became the title of an essay, "Is Theology Poetry?" In addressing this question, he makes some useful distinctions: First, he clarifies the question itself, believing it to be somewhat derogatory toward poetry. Second, Lewis offers a basic definition of poetry, one that is meant to suffice for the topic at hand—that poetry is "writing which arouses and in part satisfies the imagination."[32] So the question is really whether or not Christian theology is something we believe in because of its imaginative appeal or because it speaks truth. Lewis tends to think Christian theology is bad poetry.

Finally, Lewis makes several distinctions about the imagination. For our purposes, these are what matter most. He adds to the earlier definitions of imagination, explaining that the imagination loves to do two things: It loves to "embrace its object completely, to take it in at a single glance, and see it as something harmonious, symmetrical, and self-explanatory." It also enjoys losing "itself in a labyrinth, to surrender to the inextricable."[33] And this is something theology does not easily do. To ask if theology is *only* poetry is to ask if it is merely *mythological* (in the worst sense of the word). And here Lewis makes another key distinction when he notes that there is a difference between "imaginative enjoyment and intellectual assent."[34] From the 1300s to the 1800s, Christian Europe delighted in Greek and Roman mythologies without believing in them on any theological level. Atheists often find aesthetic pleasure in Christianity that Christians miss. Modern poets have a love for the beauty of Greek mythology that the Greeks themselves couldn't match.

Lewis is attempting to draw his audience to a distinction between believing a thing to be true and enjoying an imaginative experience, what he calls an "aesthetic effect."[35] These activities of the mind are not the same, and are not automatically joined to each other. If someone were to tell me stories of the Trojan wars, something I think more mythological than historical, it would have an aesthetic effect on me. If someone were then to tell me stories from the Napoleonic wars, which in my intellect I would take as history, it too would have an aesthetic effect on me (though Lewis says the effect would be different). The point is that aesthetic enjoyment, though it may have some relation to intellectual agreement, isn't the same thing as intellectual agreement. What happens when we reason and what happens when we imagine are different things.

Lewis emphasizes this point in an essay called "Horrid Red Things." He tells the story of overhearing a conversation between a woman and her little daughter in which the woman told the girl not to take too many aspirin or they'd be poisonous. The girl replied, "But why? . . . If you squash them you don't find any horrid red things inside them."[36] What was immediately clear was that the girl had a false image of what poison looks like; at the same time, however, she had a true understanding that poison could kill or harm. She had the right idea, but the wrong image. Recall Screwtape's ploy that the devil can't possibly be real because, after all, who could ever believe in a creature in red tights with horns and a pitchfork?[37] You can see the mistake in the thinking: the statement argues against an unbelievable image of the devil, not against the idea of a fallen angel who considers God his greatest enemy. Lewis summarizes the point: "What you think is one thing; what you imagine while you are thinking is another."[38] Lewis is more emphatic on the point in *Miracles,* where he notes that "clear *thinking*" can be accompanied by "*imagining* which is ludicrously false,"[39] but that thinking can still be sound when it is accompanied by images we know to be false—and even when it's accompanied by images we don't know to be false.[40]

But this doesn't mean they can't be connected. Lewis extends his epistemological argument in *Miracles,* noting that, while images may be false, in the case of dealing with anything that is not sensory, we *must* use imaginative language, the language of metaphor—it's the only option we have. If I *grasp* an argument or *see* the point you're making, I'm not using literal language, and the images of grasping and seeing are the best metaphors I have for saying that I understand the argument or point[41] (to *understand* is just as much a metaphor, by the way, even if we don't recognize that it is). Whenever we talk about nonsensory things, we can only talk about them using metaphors—the language of imagination.

In "Is Theology Poetry?" Lewis concludes that if we now look at the death of Balder as a myth that is untrue (in the sense that it didn't happen in history), we do not have to automatically look at the death of Christ as a myth that is untrue. Both give an aesthetic experience. But the myth of Christ can be a myth that is also historically true.[42] Furthermore, the aesthetic or mythic experience in each may yet point to a valid source of knowledge that comes to us through the imagination.

To explain this, we will have to look at yet another essay. However, to conclude this section with a point of summary and emphasis, I'd say this: Lewis is telling us that, though the imagination may have epistemological limitations, it cannot be mistaken as epistemologically worthless.

Myth, Reality, and Truth

Lewis's clearest statement regarding how experience, imagination, and myth work toward real human knowledge is probably to be found in "Myth Became Fact," where in a proposal that would seem strange to us, he connects myth to reality, but then separates reality from truth! He writes, "What flows into you from the myth is not truth but reality (truth is always about something, but reality is that *about which* truth is)."[43] Key idea: reality (or fact) is what *is*; truth is a proposition *about* fact. Next, Lewis describes our earthly existence as a "valley of separation,"[44] or abstraction, arguing that "Myth is the mountain whence all the different streams arise which become truths down here in the valley; *in hac valle abstractionis.*"[45] Lewis is saying that meaning can be abstract language statements like my explanation of Luke's internal struggle in *The Empire Strikes Back.* But it can also be experiential and can precede language.

This is an idea Lewis begins to approach in his essay "The Language of Religion." He points out that, far from being able to quantify reality in terms of the specialized languages of science or theology, most of experience can only be communicated with plain or poetic language. We may tend to think that most of what we experience can be related to others using language that is literal and precise, but Lewis thinks the opposite is true.[46] Even a theologically accurate phrase—for example, "Jesus Christ is God's Son"—is a metaphor.[47] It is true, but it is not literal. The relationship between Christ and the Father in the Trinity is not the same as the relationship between a man and his son. There was a time in which my son did not exist. Then he came into existence. But the first and second persons of the Trinity have coexisted eternally. We may attempt to convert the metaphor into a theological abstraction—for example, "There is between Jesus and God an asymmetrical, social, harmonious relation involving homogeneity"[48]—but, in doing so, the meaning will be all but lost to us. Lewis concludes that the "very essence of our life as conscious beings, all day and every day, consists of something which cannot be communicated except by hints, similes, metaphors, and the use of those emotions . . . which are pointers to it."[49] We'll soon see Lewis take this a step further with myth: that some meanings can't be communicated in language at all.

All right, let's go back to "Myth Became Fact." This essay is about many things, but it starts out being about how knowledge works. It first takes up the problem of thinking versus experiencing: to know by thought is to withdraw ourselves from reality; to know by experience is to be so caught up in the real that we can't think about it clearly. Here's an example: we can laugh at a joke or think about why it's funny, but we can't do both at the same time. Or another: Lewis says if his tooth would stop aching, he could write another chapter for his book about pain; but when the pain stops, then what does he really know about it?[50] We can't study pleasure while having sex, we can't theologize about repentance when we're practicing repentance,[51] and we can't examine humor while we're laughing hysterically. But, on the other hand, when can we really know anything about these activities except when we're doing them?[52]

In order to understand how limiting this dilemma really is, Lewis suggests we think about the myth of Orpheus and Eurydice. Orpheus was allowed to lead Eurydice out of the land of the dead by holding her hand, but the moment he tried to turn around and see her, she disappeared. If we focus on this concrete myth, the abstract concept of "thinking versus experiencing" is suddenly something we can *imagine*. If I then take what Lewis is saying and explain it in abstract, allegorical statements: *experience* is Orpheus's holding Eurydice's hand; *thinking* is her disappearing when he turns around to get a clear look at her; and the *myth*, apart from this explanation, is an image of these ideas that acts on our imaginations like an experience. Lewis goes on to note that our response might be that we've never perceived the meaning just described in the myth of Orpheus and Eurydice. To this he agrees, saying that we haven't been looking for abstract meanings in the myth in any way. If we were looking for abstract meanings in the myth, it would stop being a myth to us and become an allegory (as we have just seen). Lewis says that, in receiving the myth as a *myth*, "You were not knowing, but tasting; but what you were tasting turns out to be a universal principle. The moment we state this principle, we are admittedly back in the world of abstraction. It is only while receiving the myth as a story that you experience the principle concretely."[53] In other words, when we take a meaning out

of a myth, we turn it into an abstract statement, an idea. When
we leave the meaning in the myth and do not try to turn it into
propositional language statements, the meaning remains (or at
least mimics) a concrete experience, but it's a very special kind
of concrete experience.

It's an experience of something absolute, some Platonic idea
coming down to us from a higher reality. Go back to Lewis's
examples of humor, love, or pain. We can think about the joke,
or we can laugh at it; however, even when we're experiencing
the joke (or the pain), we are only experiencing an *instance* of
it. We can think about love, or we can experience the consummation of the marriage bed—the one is abstract, the other is
concrete—but in neither of these do we encounter love *itself*,[54]
the Platonic essence that gives all earthly love, experienced or
contemplated, its meaning. This is the "universal principle" to
which Lewis refers in "Myth Became Fact." While we are loving a person, experiencing a pain, or enjoying a pleasure, we
never actually encounter "Pleasure, Pain, or Personality." But
when we begin to apprehend them in the abstract reason, these
most concrete of realities "sink to the level of mere instances or
examples."[55] But through myth, the governing ideas of the universe can be experienced concretely. And here, then, we come
back to imagination and find at least part of its relationship to
truth in Lewis's thinking: Myth is perceived in the imagination.
It is not, foremost, a thing we decode or decipher, it's a thing
we experience; but in experiencing a great myth via the imagination, we encounter transcendent, Platonic ideas[56] that have
been transformed into earthly, concrete experiences.

Now we return to the concept of *meaning*: when we receive
myth as story, we are experiencing a principle concretely. Only
when we put the experience into words does the principle become abstract. But if we can know a principle either concretely
or by abstraction, then meaning can be either concrete or abstract.
This agrees with the statement in "Bluspels and Flalansferes"

that meaning is the necessary antecedent to truth.[57] Some meanings are abstract propositions—word statements like my explanation of the scene from *The Empire Strikes Back*. But there are other kinds of meanings, which can only be grasped in the experiential imagination. Such meanings—the kind we get in myth, for example—come prior to abstraction and apart from language. From them we do not get truths *about* reality, but rather tastes of reality *itself*.

Myth as Wordless Language

If meanings don't have to be truth statements, they also don't have to come in words. Film is again my favorite example: I can remember a time watching a movie with my daughter when she was young. The film wasn't scary per se, but it was an action film for children, and it included suspenseful moments. At one point my daughter told me she was scared. For a moment, I wondered why, and then I realized she'd seen enough movies to know unconsciously that, when a certain kind of music was playing, something "jumpy" or suspenseful was about to happen. At a young age, without consciously knowing why, my daughter had made the connection in meaning between certain kinds of music and certain actions in the plot of a movie. So nonverbal meanings can exist. And for Lewis, this is a key idea in understanding myth.

Lewis sees myth as a communication that is not in the words used to express it, but in the form of the myth itself. Lewis explains this in his collection of George MacDonald sayings, when he says that "Myth does not essentially exist in *words* at all." He thinks, for example, of the Norse myth of Balder. It's a wonderful myth, everyone agrees, but when we think of the story, what version are we thinking about—what poet has written the story down in the most beautiful verse, what words do we think of when we think of the story? Lewis's answer is we think of no specific words or version. "What really delights and nourishes me is a particular pattern of events, which would equally delight and nourish if it had reached me by some medium which involved no words at all—say by a mime, or a film."[58] In short, the meaning of a myth can be communicated apart from language.[59] As such, myth becomes a mode of *languaging* (my word), a language in and of itself apart from words. Lewis suggests this idea specifically in *A Preface to Paradise Lost*, saying, "giants, dragons, paradises, gods, and the like are themselves the expression of certain basic elements in man's spiritual experience. In that sense they are more like words—the words of a language which speaks the else unspeakable."[60]

Lewis says something similar in "On Three Ways of Writing for Children," where he talks about the significant presence of creatures, such as talking animals, giants, and dwarves, which are not human but act in human ways. He says, "I believe these to be at least . . . an admirable hieroglyphic which conveys psychology, types of character, more briefly than novelistic presentation," and he offers the example of Mr. Badger from *The Wind in the Willows*. Here we find a character whose very essence, once met by a child reader, instills a "knowledge of humanity and of English social history," which the child could not get so fully by any other means.[61]

Lewis further suggests the possibility that there are times in which the imaginative languaging of myth (where images are language) is superior to the abstracting nature of language, as he notes in his narrative poem "The Queen of Drum," where one character acknowledges that when truths become "hardened at the touch / Of language," they turn to falsehood—the language of "waking discourse" cannot achieve what dreams can.[62]

The very objects and actions of a myth—giants, enchanted forests, magical swords, dragons, escapes, underworld journeys—are the language of myth.[63] It's not the word *giant* that is the language of myth, it's the giant *itself*—its existence within the story, its presence and actions, and all the imaginative meaning that presence and action contain.[64] Myth represents a mode of thinking that turns language into a kind of concrete reality; it represents an approach to or method of thought that is very old.

Myth as Concrete Thought

George Lucas once referred to myth as "psychological archaeology."[65] In his book *Poetic Diction*, Owen Barfield argued for the possibility of an ancient mode of thought particular to myth.[66] This book had a profound influence on both Lewis's and Tolkien's ideas about myth.[67] According to Barfield, a careful study of linguistic history reveals that a strong distinction between sign and signified, between the literal and the figurative, is new to human thinking. For people before the modern era (even up through the medieval period), to name a thing was to invoke it; speech had physical consequences in the world; words were what they signified; metaphorical meanings were possible because their connective representation was in some way literal. In the past, words were more like pictures, in fact more like physical objects and actions.

In his poem "The Birth of Language," Lewis imagines words descending from Mercury's sphere to Earth in an action that begins to strip the words of their concrete being,[68] so that "Fact shrinks to truth" and words become "bony and abstract," devoid of their former glory save for brief moments when poetic verse gives a glimpse of their original potency.[69] This idea of a concreteness to language is also expressed in *That Hideous Strength*, where a character named Dimble speaks of a time closer to the Fall when "mental processes were much more like physical actions."[70] Even further back, in a time when abstract thought was not divorced from concrete action, there was the

"Great Tongue,"[71] a language described not as words that people speak, but as utterances that "speak themselves" through the person using them—words speaking "from some strong place at a distance—or as if they were not words at all but present operations of God. . . . [T]his was the language spoken before the Fall and beyond the Moon and the meanings were not given to the syllables . . . but truly inherent in them. . . . This was Language herself. . . ."[72]

Barfield suggests the metaphor "I have no stomach for that"[73] as an example of the abstract and concrete and the literal and figurative coming together. This phrase is used to express our dislike for a thing. It is figurative . . . mostly. When I say, "I have no stomach for modern art," I'm not saying I get nauseous when I look at an abstract painting. However, if I say, "I have no stomach for horror films," I am not only expressing my dislike for them, I am also saying that the blood, gore, and suspense in them *do* make me nauseous. Here is an example of a phrase that is both literal and figurative at the same time. Barfield claims humanity used to both think and use language this way constantly. Speech and action were much closer to each other than in our own day.

Again, Barfield's contention is that the history of language shows that words in the past did not begin as literal terms that later took on metaphorical meaning. On the contrary, many words taken as literal today are in fact dead metaphors (take the word *depression;* we use this word literally to denote a psychological state of extreme sadness; but the word is a metaphor—to be *pressed down*—but a dead metaphor for us since we've forgotten the symbolism and only take an abstract meaning for the word). But far in the past, as the record of words shows, the distinction between literal and figurative simply did not exist in language—and if not in language, then also not in human thinking. The earliest languages show that human beings did not have separate words for abstract ideas and concrete objects.

All words contained both literal and abstract meanings. Why did people use language this way? Because they thought this way.[74] Eventually, single meanings in language became divided into "contrasted pairs—the abstract and the concrete, particular and general, objective and subjective."[75] This happened because, again, people started thinking this way. But how is it that people thought the way they did in the past?

Barfield's answer is that "those mysterious relations between separate external objects, and between objects and feelings or ideas . . . exist independently, not indeed of Thought, but of any individual thinker."[76] There are vast relations of meaning in life itself, apart from any such relations people assign with linguistic labels. These relations exist because thought exists independent of human thinkers. Nature is permeated with meaning because it is permeated with thought. The ancient languages prove that these meanings or relationships were apprehended by people as "direct perceptual experience." They "observed a unity" and were not, therefore, aware of any relation. The relation was *not* a relation, but a reality—the objects connected or the object and idea connected were not seen as separate-but-connected; they were seen as one. But as human consciousness has developed over the centuries, Barfield claims, we have lost the power to see such unities.[77]

Lewis himself chronicles the increasing separation of thought and object from the late Middle Ages to the Romantic period. It began with a new astronomy that developed a revolution in methodology, one that emphasized mathematics to construct hypotheses that would be tested not just by simple observation, but by precisely controlled observations that could be carefully measured. Pragmatically speaking, this new approach "delivered Nature into our hands," but it also had a profound long-term effect on our thought processes—not our thoughts, but on the *way* we think. In reducing the natural world to equations and measurements, we traded an organic vision of the universe for a mechanistic one. We emptied the world "first of her indwelling spirits" like fauns and dryads, then of her mystical potencies, and finally of her "colours, smells, and tastes." We became like Midas—rich with knowledge, but everything we touched "had gone dead and cold." In the century that followed, we lost our "mythical imagination," which was replaced by the "conceit, and later the personified abstraction," until—desperate to span the chasm between our abstract knowledge and the cosmos we had stripped of its meaning—came the "Nature poetry of the Romantics."[78] Lewis further suggests in *Perelandra* that Barfield's description of ancient knowing as a unity of thinking and experiencing may have been the norm for Adam and Eve, as he describes the Green Lady's surprise response to Ransom's use of abstract reason: she wonders if it is wise to "step out of life into the Alongside and look . . . at oneself living as if one were not alive."[79]

Barfield writes that reality was "once self-evident, and therefore not conceptually experienced," but now such knowing can "only be reached by an effort of the individual mind—this is what is contained in a true poetic metaphor, and every metaphor is true."[80] Barfield explains this point in an appendix: "The distinction between true and false metaphor corresponds to the distinction between Myth and Allegory, allegory being a more or less conscious hypostatization of *ideas* . . . and myth the true child of Meaning, begotten on imagination."[81] Here we're getting to the main point of this long look into Barfield's poetics: He believes that myth, or true metaphor, is the act of perceiving a unity (of objects or an object and an idea) not as an abstract relationship, but as a concrete singularity.

Barfield illustrates by noting that poets throughout the ages have connected death with sleep and winter, and birth with waking and summer—images that are often used as metaphors for various spiritual experiences, especially the shedding of the corruptible body by the soul and its subsequent putting on of the incorruptible. Barfield then says, along the conceptual lines of a "true metaphor," that, if this concept is right, some "older, undivided 'meaning'" should exist "from which all these logically disconnected, but poetically connected ideas have sprung."[82] This is exactly what Barfield finds in the myth of Demeter and Persephone:[83] "In the myth of Demeter the ideas of waking and sleeping, of summer and winter, of life and death, of mortality and immortality are all lost in one pervasive meaning."[84] Different ideas find singular unity in myth. The connections are not logical but associative, visible in the imagination. They are varied and multiple, and so Barfield can say myth is the true child of meaning—that is, in myth there is a multiplicity of meaning.

One catches here a hint of Lewis's *The Last Battle*—that world where everything *meant* more. "Mythology," Barfield continues, "is the ghost of concrete meaning. Connections between discrete phenomena, connections which are now apprehended as metaphor, were once perceived as immediate realities."[85] This idea is echoed in another of Lewis's descriptions of a heavenly world in *The Great Divorce:* A ghostly man has come to heaven and meets a resident, an old friend, who intends to take him to the place where truth resides. But the ghost finds the idea of final answers to be stifling. The search for truth is what matters—not the finding; the finding would lead to stagnation. The heavenly being answers that the ghost thinks this because he has ever only encountered truth in the abstracting intellect. But "I will bring you where you can taste it like honey and be embraced by it as by a bridegroom."[86] Lewis seems to be suggesting that something of Barfield's description of mythic knowing, or "concrete thought," belonged to us in Eden and will belong to us again in heaven.

Let's make sure one more time that we get it: What we learn about myth from Barfield is that myth communicates holistic meaning to our immediate perceptions. It bypasses the abstracting natures of reason and language and enters immediately, intuitively into our understanding so that it is not an object containing meaning, but rather *is* concrete, experiential meaning itself. Myth allows subject to commingle with object with greater immediacy and intimacy, and it allows thinking and experiencing to occur simultaneously. The agent of this commingling in the human mind—the place into which myth can enter with immediate, intuitive understanding—is the imagination.

I keep coming back to movie illustrations in this chapter because of the similarities between myth (as Lewis understood it) and film. Doing so one more time, by way of conclusion, may make some of these difficult ideas easier to understand. Just as myth is a form of languaging and an expression of concrete thought, so film too is a mode of languaging that communicates to us like a physical action, as a concrete experience; it is able to do so either without language or by converting language into experiential form.

An example of film communicating as form-without-word can be seen in *Edward Scissorhands,* one of Tim Burton's early movies. In the middle of the movie, we see a long shot of the street on which Edward's adoptive family lives. Husbands simultaneously walk out to their cars from the various homes, heading off for the day. They get in their cars at the same time, pull out of their driveways at the same time, and drive off (after a bit of hesitation and jockeying for road space) at the same time. There are no words, only pleasant, *Leave It to Beaver*-esque music. But here's what's really strange: the houses and the cars are all painted pastel colors. From a greater distance the street might look like an Easter basket. The colors are all solid, no two-tones: whole houses and cars painted pink, or blue, or yellow, or green pastel.[87] Actions, sights, and sounds—all of them deliberate, intended. And without language, meaning is communicated in this scene. We certainly *can,* in this instance, put the meaning into words: "Suburbia is a world of conformity and facade." But the point is that we get the meaning without having to put it into words. Film communicates in a mythic fashion, often with meanings that simply can't be abstracted into words.

One more example: Think of some favorite song, the kind that "blows you away" the first time you hear it. It moves you. You connect to it. It evokes feelings and thoughts you can't quite describe. Recall next how a month or two (or six) later you actually bother to pay attention to the lyrics, and you finally figure out what the song was saying. In one sense you knew all along what the song was about. You understood meanings in it that couldn't be put into words—meanings in the music itself or in the way a certain phrase touched your heart or connected with memories. The analysis of the lyrics was your reasoning-self becoming aware of abstract, propositional meanings that your experiential-self had not encountered. To use Lewis's terminology, you first *tasted* the song, then you came to *know* it. But to abandon the taste—the meanings that still cannot be put into words even after some analysis—is to abandon meanings that are certainly there. In short, myth represents a way of thinking, a mode of knowing, a method of languaging that may be closer to the way humanity thought, knew, and spoke before the Fall and for some centuries thereafter. Perhaps myth even shows us a glimpse of the kind of knowledge and communication we will have and do in heaven.

In this book's introduction I raised a question that called for an answer: Why do we love and even need myth so much? The answer seems to be that we were meant for it. At the same time, I've offered a caution in this chapter regarding the limitations of myth and imagination. However we use myth to reveal truth, others will use it to conceal lies *within* mythic truth; in the fallen world in which we find ourselves, mythic and imaginative knowledge will have to be checked against reason, not because the latter is superior, but because the concrete and the abstract have been split in human knowing, and it's the only way we can come close to any kind of complete knowledge down here in the valley of separation.

Still, an understanding of the connection between myth and epistemology can provide some much-needed tools for something C. S. Lewis cared greatly about: reaching the lost and teaching the saved. If mythic thinking is central to human nature, then giving thought to how we can use mythic discourse for the sake of God's Kingdom and how we can avoid and combat the misuses of it in our culture is important. It's equally important that we consider how a mythic mode of thought might have us rethink our approaches to scriptural interpretation. How can we use story to reach people? What's the most effective kind of storytelling? How might the kind of thinking with which we approach our reading of the Bible be skewed for a lack of mythic understanding? How should we be interpreting scripture in ways that incorporate this most ancient form of thought?

The answers to those questions are for another book, likely written by someone else, but I hope it spurs its readers to consider how understanding myth can be converted into acts of love. The bottom line is that we need such a response, because myth will always be with us. This is probably a good thing, because, as Lewis puts it, "A great myth is relevant as long as the predicament of humanity lasts; as long as humanity lasts. It will always work, on those who can receive it, the same catharsis."[88]

CHAPTER ELEVEN

Lewis and the North

No study of Lewis's theory of myth can be complete without taking some time to discuss the importance of Norse mythology in his life. Perusing Mr. Tumnus's bookshelf, with its emphasis on Greek mythology, didn't really allow us to look at this area of Lewis's mythic interest, but covering it is a must—it was too important to him not to. His work in medieval and Renaissance studies made Lewis more apt to write about the Greek myths as he encountered them in Western literature. However, while he liked Greek myth as well as the myths of several other cultures, what Lewis best loved was Norse myth. In it he found some of his earliest and deepest encounters with joy, a voice with which to begin narrative writing, a new love for nature, lifelong friendships with Arthur Greeves and J. R. R. Tolkien, and a doorway that would lead him to his belief in Christ as the myth that became fact.

Longing and the Northern Call

In chapters 6 and 9 we looked at the theme of longing, as it appears in Lewis's life. For years he was haunted by a desire for some nameless thing that he thought he would find in one source or another—in nature, in romance, in fantastic literature, especially myth, and most especially in Norse myth. But all of these turned out to be mere shadows of the transcendent "other"—that is, God—which he would ultimately recognize as the true source of his longing. Early on, however, when he encountered transcendent desire, the longing was accompanied by such intense, sweet pleasure that Lewis named it "joy." He found that joy, though an unfulfilled desire, was a greater pleasure than any fulfilled desires he might experience in any other part of his life.

Lewis's first encounters with joy occurred at a very young age and preceded his discovery of Norse mythology. But when Norse myth did enter his experience, the joy he felt was the greatest he'd ever known. It happened when Lewis was only around nine years old.[1] He says he was casually turning the pages in a collection of Longfellow when he came across the American poet's translation of "Tegnér's Drapa." There he read just the first three lines of the poem: "I heard a voice, that cried, / 'Balder the Beautiful / Is dead, is dead!'"[2] Lewis then says that, though he knew nothing of Balder at that time, he was immediately "uplifted into huge regions of northern sky," which created in him a desire he could not describe.[3] It is after relating this event in his autobiography that Lewis defines what he means by joy. Later in the book he says that reading works of Norse myth, over and over again, stabbed him with joy,[4] and that the Norse gods gave Lewis his first taste of the glory of God, which joy had made him pursue his entire life.[5]

Lewis describes another intense experience of joy through Norse myth, which occurred four years later, when he was around thirteen.[6] This instance also occurred by chance and the turn of a page. Lewis was looking at a periodical featuring book advertisements, when his eyes fell on the title *Siegfried and the Twilight of the Gods* and a picture from an edition of this book, which was illustrated by Arthur Rackham.[7] Lewis says he knew nothing of Wagner or Siegfried at that time and had no idea what the "Twilight of the Gods" referred to. But he writes that "Pure 'Northernness' engulfed me: a vision of huge, clear spaces hanging above the Atlantic in the endless twilight of Northern summer, remoteness, severity."[8] He immediately realized that he had encountered this mythic vision before in "Tegnér's Drapa"—that Siegfried belonged to the world from which Balder also came. He also realized that he had had another experience of joy and that experiencing it again became the most important desire of his life. Joy then became Lewis's chief pursuit throughout his teens and twenties, a pursuit that would eventually lead him to God.

During those earliest years, especially, Northernness seemed to Lewis more important than the religion of his youth. He felt a worshipful awe for the Norse gods he didn't believe in, more so than he had ever felt for God when he had believed in Him as a boy.[9] This adoration never caused Lewis to believe in the Northern gods (as he puts it, he "never mistook imagination for reality"[10] in their regard). Northernness simply raised a desire for an object that was absent from his experience. He would continue to pursue that object till he found it. In other words, C. S. Lewis's rapturous love for Norse myth contributed to his conversion to Christianity.

Other Lewis Norse-i-ties

Lewis's passion for the North influenced other areas of his life as well. Soon after his encounter with the story of Siegfried and the Niblung, as he learned it from Wagner's *Der Ring des Nibelungen,* he began his own heroic poem recounting the story. Though he didn't finish his tale, he wrote 801 lines in rhyming heroic couplets, a remarkable feat for a boy of thirteen or fourteen.[11] More importantly, according to Lewis, this work taught him what the act of writing really meant,[12] and he continued in the pursuit of that act the rest of his life. This included writing another Norse tale. On October 6, 1914, Lewis sent a letter[13] to Arthur Greeves in which he outlined, at some length and in six parts, a tragedy he hoped to write after the fashion of *Prometheus Bound*, but about the Norse god Loki, who would be the hero of Lewis's story. Lewis hoped his friend Arthur could set music to the tale, turning it into an opera. The title of this tragic poem is "Loki Bound," but though Lewis finished the poem, only 121 lines have survived.[14]

Norse mythology did more than take Lewis into a world of books. It took him out into his beloved nature. For a while, Lewis's encounters in nature reminded him of the joy he experienced from books of Norse myth. But then nature herself began to give Lewis stabs of joy as well.[15] Norse myth enchanted nature for Lewis, and the enchantment remained with him all his life.

Lewis's love of Norse myth also meant the creation of two significant friendships. The first of these was with Arthur Greeves. In 1914 Lewis was asked to go visit a neighbor who was in bed convalescing. Uncharacteristically, he accepted the invitation. He writes that he found Arthur sitting up in his bed and immediately noticed that on the night table lay a copy of the book *Myths of the Norsemen*. Upon learning that they both loved Norse myth, the boys immediately had the book up in their hands, their heads bent over the pages. The conversation that followed was torrential, and Lewis discovered that Arthur Greeves knew the same encounters with longing that he knew and that Greeves, like Lewis, had encountered it in Norse myth.[16] Thereafter, Greeves became one of Lewis's lifelong friends.

The second significant friendship was with J. R. R. Tolkien. Lewis's love for Norse myth made him pursue it to the point of developing some expertise in the subject.[17] But that expertise was limited (in Lewis's thinking) by a lack of training in the language of Old Icelandic (or Old Norse). Lewis continued his pursuit of Norse mythology by joining a group in 1927 called the Coalbiters, an Oxford club that Tolkien had started, whose purpose was reading the sagas and Eddur in their original language.[18] Lewis wrote to Arthur Greeves of reading the *Younger Edda* and the *Völsunga Saga*.[19] The Coalbiters would eventually give way to the Inklings, the literary group that had a profound effect on both Tolkien's and Lewis's writings. Through their mutual love for Norse mythology, Tolkien and Lewis began a friendship that would impact them both. As noted in chapter 7, an important conversation with Tolkien and Hugo Dyson on the truth-value of myth laid the last stone in Lewis's road to Christianity. It is additionally true, according to Tolkien, that except for Lewis's constant encouragement he might have never finished or tried to publish *The Lord of the Rings*.[20] Once, when asked about similarities between their works, Lewis replied that he and Tolkien were "both soaked in Norse mythology."[21] It is not an exaggeration to say that, without their mutual love of Norse myth, Lewis and Tolkien might not have become friends;[22] Lewis might not have become a Christian; and Tolkien might not have completed his greatest Middle-earth saga.

Finally some notes on Norse myth in Lewis's writings. A few references to the Norse gods have already appeared in this book. Though Lewis loved Norse myth, however, he didn't write much about it. There is the essay "First and Second Things," which we looked at briefly in chapter 8. In that essay Lewis expresses the same love for Norse myth that he shares with us in *Surprised by Joy*. This is the essay in which he further attacks the Nazis for their failure to understand the essence of Norse myth.[23] Lewis briefly discusses the Norse view of time in his essay "Historicism."[24] And, though it is unfortunately difficult to find, the American edition of *The Lion, the Witch and the Wardrobe* contains a few revisions by Lewis that add some Norse elements to the book's blending of myths. The captain of the White Witch's secret police, a wolf named Maugrim,[25] undergoes a name change in the American edition, where he is called Fenris Ulf,[26] after a monstrous wolf from Norse mythology.[27] And the Secret Hill,

with its fire-stones on which the deep magic is written,[28] becomes, in the American edition, the World Ash Tree,[29] a reference to the great tree Yggdrasil, which holds up the earth and
connects all the realms of Norse mythology.[30]

Surprisingly, two new sources of Lewis writing on Norse myth
have emerged in the last few years. The first of these was mentioned in chapter 7. Part of the "Mythonomy" fragment contains
a paragraph contrasting Zeus and Odin, the key difference being
Odin's mortality: he is bound in time and suffers its effects. He
is less like the Greek gods and more like Ulysses, but even that
man has his homecoming, while Odin's end is death and defeat.
He is one who fights with his back up against a wall.[31] Lewis
concludes the fragment saying Odin best represents the idea (expressed in an ancient English text) that hearts will grow bolder,
and spirits will grow stronger as strength fails us.[32]

More recently, Lewis's love of Norse mythology has linked
him to a career as a spy for the British Secret Service in World
War II. This is not quite the case, but a discovery by Harry Lee
Poe has revealed an interesting connection.[33] While browsing
eBay, Poe ran across a vinyl audio recording (two of four sides)
of Lewis presenting a talk entitled, "The Norse Spirit in English Literature." The eBay dealer from whom Poe obtained the
record lives in Iceland. This talk was lost to Lewis scholarship
and has yet to be published in print form, and only a few have
heard its content so far.

The interesting connection to the spy world is that Lewis was
asked to make the record in 1941 by the Joint Broadcasting Committee, which was actually an arm of the British secret intelligence. In May 1940, to halt the progress of the Nazis through Europe, British armed forces invaded Iceland, which would prove
to be a strategic position for watching over the North Atlantic
by air. In order to keep the good will of the people of Iceland,
the committee asked Lewis to record a message to them—essentially, a propaganda piece. In the recording, Lewis emphasizes an

affinity the British people have with Iceland through the influences of her literature and language on the literature of Britain. Lewis also mentions his personal love for Icelandic language and Norse literature. A more thorough discussion of the content of the recording is available in Poe's article; otherwise, we will have to wait till the recording's print publication (and hopefully the eventual discovery of the missing second record) to know the full content of Lewis's message to the men of the North.

Finally, the most powerful point Lewis makes with any reference to Norse mythology occurs in his foreword to Joy Davidman's *Smoke on the Mountain.* Lewis writes that the flaw in modern Western culture that Davidman points out so well is that of fear, by which he means simply "cowardice."[34] And while he hopes that the people of England and America, if faced with a need for courage, would rise up to meet it, he has his doubts and argues the sober truth that, if such courage is not to be found, Western civilization will have to confess that two thousand years of Christian influence have not raised us to the "level of the Stoics and Vikings." The worst that a Christian has to face is to die for Christ and rise in Him, but the Vikings were willing to die and *not* rise with Odin.[35]

CHAPTER TWELVE

An Interpretive Mystery
of Mythic Proportion

I've been holding out on you—trying to avoid a problem. It's not a profound one, but it is a puzzle, and
who doesn't love a puzzle to solve? I've presented to
you a wonderfully cohesive, overarching view of Lewis's theory
of myth that appears complete, unified, and without contradiction. But there *is* a contradiction, or at least the appearance
of one.

Many people are familiar with Lewis's second attempt at
writing the story of his conversion, *The Pilgrim's Regress,* and
his third attempt, *Surprised by Joy.* But fewer are familiar with
his first attempt. This short document (twenty-eight pages in
print), given the name "Early Prose Joy" by Walter Hooper, was
first published in 2013, introduced and transcribed (with notes)
by Andrew Lazo, in volume 30 of the journal *VII.*[1] Lewis wrote
"Early Prose Joy" after his conversion to theism in the summer of 1930 but before his conversion to Christianity in the fall
of 1931. Near the end of the text, Lewis is struggling with, but
coming close to belief in God. He writes, "Vainly I pleaded that
if I *addressed* God, making Him another soul over against my
soul, when He was really the ground of souls, I should be using a mythology. The answer was too plain. 'Child, if you will,
it *is* mythology. *It is truth, not fact: an image not the very real.* But
it is *My* mythology—the symbol under which I offer Myself to

you.'"[2] The italicized sentence and the first clause after it appear with slight additions in *The Pilgrim's Regress* at the moment the main character is coming to believe not just in God, but in the church[3] (and that's only one complication we face with this text). But the passage that appears to contradict this one was written over a decade later in "Myth Became Fact." We saw it in chapter 10: "What *flows into you from the myth is not truth but reality* (truth is always about something, but reality is that *about which* truth is)."[4] Let's look at the key passages side by side:

> "Early Prose Joy": "it *is* mythology. It is truth, not fact: an image not the very real."
>
> "Myth Became Fact": "What flows into you from the myth is not truth but reality. . . ."

In the first text we seem to be reading that myth is truth, not fact. In the second text we seem to be reading that myth is fact, not truth.

Now, if we were going to do this right, we'd probably need another book here, one on Lewis's view of *fact* and *truth*.[5] Still, with the thorough look we've taken at Lewis's ideas on myth, I think we can come to a possible conclusion about the passages at hand, one that eliminates the contradictions.[6]

Let's first consider some options that *might* explain the contradictory passages:

1. Lewis's ideas on myth, truth, and fact evolved over the years, and the change is reflected in the difference between the early texts and the later one. But if so, which ideas about which of the three terms changed? Was it his thinking on *fact, truth,* or *myth* that changed?
2. Lewis was being sloppy with his language. The ideas are essentially the same, but the language choice in the earlier texts is inconsistent with his later comments on myth.

3. It's a matter of context: both passages are saying the same thing; when they are seen in their separate contexts, the contradictions disappear.

And finally let's also consider some potential interpretive problems:

1. Might fact and reality in Lewis's thinking be different concepts? How might this affect our understanding of the term *fact* as it appears in these passages?
2. In "Early Prose Joy," Lewis is talking about his theistic conversion; in *The Pilgrim's Regress* he uses the same words, but in the context of his Christian conversion. Does this contextual change affect what the words mean to us?
3. What is the antecedent of *it* in the statement "it *is* mythology," which appears in both "Early Prose Joy" and *The Pilgrim's Regress?* Does the word in both works refer to the same thing?[7]
4. Whatever we say about the distinctions among *fact, truth,* and *myth* as we talk about these passages, Lewis suggested in *Perelandra* that in some unfallen realm the distinctions disappear. You'll recall the passage we looked at in chapter 5, where Ransom was starting to realize that the distinction of "truth from myth and of both from fact"[8] had no meaning outside our fallen world.

These, then, are the pieces of the puzzle. But rather than cover every interpretive option, I'm going to offer my own explanation for the contradiction, leaving a thorough study of the possibilities to those of you who want to fit the puzzle together for yourselves. In "Myth Became Fact," Lewis is saying that myth shows us a higher, transcendent reality, a heavenly reality that gives meaning and order to the creation in which we live. Truth, in this essay, is about abstract thinking, which is to say that truth occurs whenever what we think *about* reality actually corresponds *to* reality. Truth is not reality in "Myth Became Fact"; rather, it is what is occurring when our thoughts about reality are accurate.

Now consider, again, two key passages. The first is from "Early Prose Joy": "Vainly I pleaded that if I *addressed* God, making Him another soul over against my soul, when He was really the ground of souls, I should be using a mythology. The answer was too plain. 'Child, if you will, it *is* mythology. . . . But it is *My* mythology.'"[9] Notice the focus on thinking about God in this passage. Lewis gets to a point where he realizes that to think about God in any *personal* sense is to think about Him mythologically.[10] But God replies that a myth—one made by God—is the only way any human being can ultimately think about Him. This reading is suggested as the passage in "Early Prose Joy" continues:

> But it is *My* mythology—the symbol under which I offer Myself to you. What else do you look to have? Have the wise Pagans not told you the story of Semele?[11] No man has seen my face and lived. Do you not think that I know, better than you, the range of your faculties, and which of the concepts and images within your power can best show forth to you as much of Me as can be shown? I made your thinking and your imagining, and do I not know how to use them? If you turn from these to some philosophy of your own invention, you are not exchanging symbol for truth: you are but choosing your myth instead of Mine.[12]

Lewis seems to be saying that there comes a point where you can no longer get at the truth about God through abstract philosophy, you can only get at it through a myth—God's chosen myth.[13] But in the next passage we need to look at, Lewis may also be saying that even myth falls short when it comes to understanding the nature of God.

We have seen this next passage before. It is from Lewis's letter of October 18, 1931: "Christianity is God expressing Himself through what we call 'real things'. Therefore it is *true*, not in the sense of being a 'description' of God (that no finite mind could take in) but in the sense of being the way in which God chooses to (or can) appear to our faculties."[14] In both of these passages, the focus is on God Himself—His essence, His nature. I would therefore argue this explanation: the passages in question do not contradict each other at all, but "Early Prose Joy" and *The Pilgrim's Regress* do reveal a limitation on myth. Normally, when myth is at its best, it shows us higher reality; truth is abstract, and is only *about* reality. But in the case of God Himself, myth itself falls short—it also becomes an abstraction! Myth may show us higher, transcendent reality, but when it deals with God, it takes a step back—it cannot show us the most *real* Reality there is—it can only show us something *about* God (and so myth becomes an abstraction, even if it is presenting God to us in images rather than ideas). What myth gives, in all of its concreteness, is merely another abstraction (and therefore a truth) when it tries to give us God. It gives us an image, but not the very real. Only in the Incarnation does myth truly meet fact when it comes to our ability to know and see God Himself. In other words, there is one situation in which myth cannot show us the *real*, but can only offer us *truth*—this is any myth that attempts to describe God, even God as He manifested Himself in history (as recorded in scripture) up to the Incarnation.

In short, my explanation for the apparent contradiction between "Early Prose Joy" and *The Pilgrim's Regress,* on the one hand, and "Myth Became Fact," on the other, is that there is no contradiction. There is instead an important exception:

1. Myth shows us reality *except* when it tries to show us God. Then it can only show us truth, and the clearest, most complete myth shown will occur when the myth is the one given to us by God.

2. The exception (to this exception) is in the Incarnation, when God becomes man. Then myth *becomes* fact—the most real thing there is.

That then is my solution to the puzzle. I leave further exploration to all who, like me, have delighted in Lewis's ideas. What began with a casual perusal of the nonexistent works on a fictional faun's bookshelf ends with what I hope is a thorough vision of C. S. Lewis's theory of myth. Or, if I might conjure up a more mythical conclusion, all books end and this one must too, but that serves to remind us of the exception: the book Lewis told us about at the end of *The Last Battle,* the one in which this life is only the cover and the title page, the book in which our own story is better than it's ever been, and every chapter in it is better than the ones that come before.

Permissions Acknowledgments

All extracts by C. S. Lewis copyright © C. S. Lewis Pte. Ltd. Reprinted by permission. "Two Pieces from C. S. Lewis's 'Moral Good' Manuscript: A First Publication" originally appeared in *VII: Journal of the Marion E. Wade Center,* volume 31 (copyright 2014). Extracts are reprinted here with permission from the Marion E. Wade Center, Wheaton College, Wheaton, IL. Part of this essay, "Mythonomy," printed by permission of the Marion E. Wade Center as owner of the manuscript. An unpublished letter of September 29, 1956, which is owned by the Lanier Theological Library, Houston TX, is quoted with the generous permission of the Lanier. Portions of several essays and chapters I've written over the last two decades appear with permission of the original publishers. These include the following: "So How *Should* We Teach English?" *Contemporary Perspectives on C. S. Lewis' The Abolition of Man: History, Philosophy, Education and Science.* Ed. Gayne Anacker and Timothy Mosteller. New York: Bloomsbury, 2017. "Meaning, Meanings and Epistemology in C. S. Lewis." *Mythlore: A Journal of J. R. R. Tolkien, C. S. Lewis, Charles Williams, and Mythopoeic Literature.* Ed. Janet B. Croft. Ohio University Press, 2007. "Faith without Film is Dull: C. S. Lewis Corrects Evangelicals on Art, Movies, and Worldview Analysis." *Christian Scholar's Review: Theme Issue: Reel Presence.* Ed. Don W. King, S. Bradley Shaw, and Craig Detweiler. XL:4 Summer 2011. "Signs and C. S. Lewis: The

Meaning of Meaning, How Hobbits Are Real, and the Value of Film." *CSL: The Bulletin of the New York C. S. Lewis Society*. Ed. Robert Trexler. New York: New York C. S. Lewis Society, 2004. "C. S. Lewis's Theory of Myth and Meaning: An Approach to the Arts." *Integrite: A Faith and Learning Journal*. Ed. John Han. vol. 5, no. 2 (Fall 2006). "Aesthetics vs. Anesthesia: C. S. Lewis on the Purpose of Art." *C. S. Lewis and the Arts: Creativity in the Shadowlands*. Baltimore: Square Halo Books, 2013. *"The Silver Chair* and the Silver Screen: C. S. Lewis on Myth, Fairy Tale and Film." *Revisiting Narnia: Fantasy, Myth and Religion in C. S. Lewis' Chronicles*. Ed. Shanna Caughey. Dallas: Benbella Books, 2005. "Aesthetics vs. Anesthesia: C. S. Lewis on the Purpose of Art." *Inklings Forever, Volume VII: A Collection of Essays Presented at the Seventh Frances White Ewbank Colloquium on C. S. Lewis and Friends, Taylor University*, 2010. "Signs and C. S. Lewis: The Meaning of *Meaning* and the Value of Film." *Inklings Forever, Volume V: A Collection of Essays Presented at the Fifth Frances White Ewbank Colloquium on C. S. Lewis and Friends, Taylor University*, 2006.

Notes

Introduction

1. Lewis, *The Lion, the Witch and the Wardrobe*, 15.

2. Walter Hooper's editor's note in Lewis, *The Collected Letters of C. S. Lewis*, vol. 2 (hereafter *CL II*), 1041, quoting from Hooper and Roger Lancelyn Green, *C. S. Lewis: A Biography* (New York: Harcourt, Brace, Jovanovich, 1974).

3. See Shippey, *J. R. R. Tolkien*, xvii–xviv.

4. As noted in numerous sources, including Seabrook, "Why Is the Force Still with Us?"

1. Of the Making of Many (Fake) Books

1. Lewis, *Surprised by Joy*, 10.

2. Lewis, *Prince Caspian*, 48.

3. Or perhaps the study of any topic is torturous if the tutor or author is himself dusty, slow, and dry. According to Paul Ford's *Companion to Narnia*, Lewis may be making an allusion to a pair of novels by Sir Walter Scott (including *Ivanhoe*) that are dedicated to the fictitious Dr. Jonas Dryasdust (85).

4. Lewis, *That Hideous Strength*, 187.

5. A philologist studies language, the origins of language, and the history of languages—especially how they change over time.

6. Lewis, *Perelandra*, 22.

7. Lewis, *Out of the Silent Planet*, 56.

8. Lewis, *Out of the Silent Planet*, 150.

9. The complete original introduction is housed along with an original typescript of *The Screwtape Letters* at the Marion E. Wade Center at

Wheaton College, Wheaton, Illinois. It was first published by Brenton Dickieson in "The Unpublished Preface to C. S. Lewis' *The Screwtape Letters*," 296–98.

10. Lewis, *Out of the Silent Planet*, 150.

11. Lewis, *Out of the Silent Planet*, 150

12. Lewis, *Out of the Silent Planet*, 150–51.

13. Lewis, *Out of the Silent Planet*, 151.

14. Lewis, *Out of the Silent Planet*, 152.

15. Lewis, *Out of the Silent Planet*, 153.

16. See Lewis's explanation to Sister Penelope in his letter to her of July or August 9, 1939, in *CL II*, 261.

17. As Lewis admits in a letter of Februrary 8, 1950, in Lewis, *The Collected Letters of C. S. Lewis*, vol. 3 (hereafter *CL III*), 11.

18. Lewis, *Perelandra*, 17.

19. See Walter Hooper's introduction to Lewis, *The Collected Poems of C. S. Lewis*, xvi.

20. Lewis, "Fern-seed and Elephants," 109.

21. Lewis, "Fern-seed and Elephants," 111.

22. Lewis, *The Voyage of the Dawn Treader*, 2.

23. Lewis, *The Voyage of the Dawn Treader*, 92.

24. See Lewis, *The Voyage of the Dawn Treader*, 109–10.

25. Lewis, *The Voyage of the Dawn Treader*, 160.

26. See Lewis, *The Voyage of the Dawn Treader*, 162–68.

27. Lewis, *The Silver Chair*, 135.

28. Lewis, *The Horse and His Boy*, 3.

29. Lewis, *Out of the Silent Planet*, 67.

30. Lewis, *Out of the Silent Planet*, 101.

31. Lewis, *That Hideous Strength*, 63.

32. Lewis, *The Great Divorce*, 36.

33. Lewis, *Till We Have Faces*, 232. For a study of these book titles, see Myers, "Browsing the Glome Library."

34. The essay is in Lewis, *God in the Dock*, 301–3.

35. In Lewis, "Bulverism," 42–45.

36. Lewis, "Bulverism," 43.

37. Lewis, *The Abolition of Man*, 13.

38. Lewis, "Myth Became Fact," 63.

39. For an in-depth look at Lewis's attempts to write about prayer, see Mead, "*Letters to Malcolm*: C. S. Lewis on Prayer," 209–35, in volume 3 of Bruce Edwards's excellent work, *C. S. Lewis: Life, Works, and Legacy*.

40. Lewis, "From Johnson's *Life of Fox*."

41. The unpublished postscript that belongs to the letter of March 22, 1932, is given a title by Lewis: "Commentary on LEWIS Ad Familiares Epist XXXVII." The original is in the collection of Lewis's letters at the Marion E. Wade Center, Wheaton College, under call number CSL / L-Barfield 28. The quotation here is from the second paragraph.

42. See Lewis, "Commentary on *The Lay of Leithian.*"

43. Tolkien, *The Fellowship of the Ring,* 1.

44. Lewis, *That Hideous Strength,* 269–70. There Lewis misspells it "Numinor."

45. Many of the above examples of Lewis's fake books and names were supplied by a host of Lewis scholars and enthusiasts who answered my call for help, including Arend Smilde, Michael Ward, Andrew Lazo, Jonathan Himes, Laura Schmidt, Charles A. Huttar, and Devin Brown, who also directed me to Peter Schakel's list of nonexistent Lewis books in chapter 2 of his *Imagination and the Arts in C. S. Lewis.* My thanks to them all.

46. Frye, *Anatomy of Criticism,* 117.

47. Lewis, "The Hobbit," 81.

48. Lewis, "On Science-Fiction," 64.

49. Lewis, "On Science-Fiction," 67.

50. Lewis, "Tolkien's *The Lord of the Rings,*" 86.

51. Lewis, "On Three Ways of Writing for Children," 27.

52. Lewis, "Tolkien's *The Lord of the Rings,*" 83.

53. Lewis, "Tolkien's *The Lord of the Rings,*" 84.

54. Tolkien, "On Fairy-Stories," 60.

55. Tolkien, "On Fairy-Stories," 68.

56. Tolkien, "Mythopoeia," lines 46–47.

57. See Tolkien, "Mythopoeia," lines 55–64.

2. Fauns and Their Fantasies

1. Lewis, "It All Began with a Picture," 42. See additional examples in Lewis, "Sometimes Fairy Stories May Say Best What's To Be Said," 36, and a letter to Cynthia Donnelly of August 15, 1954, in *CL III,* 503.

2. Ford, *Companion to Narnia,* 428.

3. Lewis, *Prince Caspian,* 86.

4. Ford, *Companion to Narnia,* 183.

5. For the remaining names, see Ford, *Companion to Narnia,* 183–84. Regarding the theme of lying, see also Lewis's poem "The Satyr," which I talk about in chapter 7.

6. Lewis, *The Lion, the Witch and the Wardrobe*, 8.

7. Lewis, *Prince Caspian*, 86.

8. See Christopher, "C. S. Lewis's Two Satyrs," 83.

9. Lewis, *Till We Have Faces*, 48.

10. Lewis, *Till We Have Faces*, 50.

11. Lewis, *Mere Christianity*, 139.

12. Lewis, *Mere Christianity*, 140.

13. Lewis, *Mere Christianity*, 151.

14. Lewis, *The Allegory of Love*, 95.

15. Lewis, *The Allegory of Love*, 95.

16. Lewis, *The Discarded Image*, 122. Capella is quoted from *De Nuptiis Mercurii et Philologiae*, II.167.

17. Lewis, *The Discarded Image*, 125.

18. Lewis, "Religion and Rocketry," 91–92.

19. Morford and Lenardon, *Classical Mythology*, 476–77.

20. Lewis, *Spenser's Images of Life*, 77.

21. Lewis, *Spenser's Images of Life*, 78.

22. See Lewis, "Period Criticism," 487–88.

23. Lewis, *The Lion, the Witch and the Wardrobe*, 17.

24. Morford and Lenardon, *Classical Mythology*, 222–23.

25. See Lewis, *The Horse and His Boy*, 71–77.

26. Lewis, *The Horse and His Boy*, 235.

27. Morford and Lenardon, *Classical Mythology*, 175–76.

28. It's worth noting that, in a letter to his friend Roger Lancelyn Green (who would become one of Lewis's official biographers), Lewis praised Green for his book *The Searching Satyrs*, which Green had translated from surviving fragments of the play written by Sophocles. See the letter of December 13, 1952, in *CL III*, 264.

29. Morford and Lenardon, *Classical Mythology*, 216–17.

30. Lewis, *The Allegory of Love*, 335.

31. See John 10:10.

32. Lewis, "On Three Ways of Writing for Children," 22.

33. The literary group hosted by Lewis, which included Lewis; his brother; Tolkien; Tolkien's son, Christopher; Owen Barfield; Charles Williams; and others.

34. See Lewis's letter of March 2, 1948, to Warfield Firor in *CL II*, 836.

35. The "Ham Testimonial" letter of March 11, 1948, in *CL II*, 839, which was sent to Firor with the letter of the following day, March 12, in *CL II*, 838.

3. Might Myth Be Real?

1. Lewis, "Forms of Things Unknown," 124–32.
2. Lewis, *The Voyage of the Dawn Treader,* 251.
3. Lewis, *Out of the Silent Planet,* 144.
4. Lewis, *Perelandra,* 40.
5. Lewis, *Perelandra,* 42.
6. Lewis, *Perelandra,* 122.
7. Lewis, *Perelandra,* 88.
8. Lewis, *Perelandra,* 172–73.
9. Lewis, *Perelandra,* 173.
10. See Lewis, *The Screwtape Letters,* 1–2.
11. Lewis, *The Pilgrim's Regress,* 154.
12. Lewis, *The Pilgrim's Regress,* 154 sidenote. The original copy containing Lewis's handwritten notes is now housed at the Marion E. Wade Center in Wheaton, Illinois; the annotated edition, edited by David C. Downing and published by the Wade Center in 2014, includes both Lewis's notes and additional annotations by Downing.
13. Lewis, *Mere Christianity,* 44.
14. I cover this topic more thoroughly in chapters 7 and 10.
15. Lewis, "Miracles," 10.
16. See also chapter 2 of Lewis, *Miracles,* 12–19. Lewis also distinguishes between uncreated Supernature (God) and created Supernature (the angels).
17. See also Lewis's image of a parallel universe in his novel fragment "The Dark Tower."
18. Lewis, *The Magician's Nephew,* 39.
19. Lewis, *The Great Divorce,* 20.
20. Lewis, *The Great Divorce,* 138.
21. Lewis, *The Last Battle,* 211.
22. Lewis, *The Last Battle,* 212.
23. Lewis, *The Last Battle,* 213.
24. Lewis, *The Last Battle,* 213.
25. Lewis, *The Last Battle,* 212.
26. Lewis, *The Last Battle,* 228.

4. *The Life and Letters of Silenus*

1. See Lewis, *The Allegory of Love,* 52. Lewis uses both forms of the god's name in his works, although the Roman form seems predominant. In this discussion, I use the two forms interchangeably, depending on context. When all else is equal, I use the Roman form.

2. Lewis, *The Allegory of Love*, 6.

3. Lewis, *The Allegory of Love*, 52.

4. Lewis, "Hamlet," 90.

5. Lewis, *English Literature in the Sixteenth Century*, 417.

6. Lewis, *English Literature in the Sixteenth Century*, 416.

7. Letter to Arthur Greeves of July 1, 1930, in Lewis, *The Collected Letters of C. S. Lewis*, vol. 1 (hereafter *CL I*), 912–13.

8. Lewis, "The Psalms," 123.

9. Lewis, "First and Second Things," 654.

10. Lewis, *The Pilgrim's Regress*, 175.

11. Lewis, *Till We Have Faces*, 284.

12. See Exodus 33:18–23 (NIV).

13. Exodus 34:29–35.

14. Lewis, *The Lion, the Witch and the Wardrobe*, 140.

15. Lewis, *Out of the Silent Planet*, 31.

16. Lewis, *Out of the Silent Planet*, 34.

17. Lewis, *Out of the Silent Planet*, 145.

18. Lewis, *Till We Have Faces*, 307–8.

19. Lewis, "The Weight of Glory," 16.

20. Ford, *Companion to Narnia*, 383.

21. Morford and Lenardon, *Classical Mythology*, 217.

22. Lewis, *The Lion, the Witch and the Wardrobe*, 16–17.

23. Lewis, *The Lion, the Witch and the Wardrobe*, 191.

24. Letter to Dom Bede Griffiths of April 15, 1947, in *CL II*, 770.

25. Morford and Lenardon, *Classical Mythology*, 217–18.

26. Lewis, *Miracles*, 179.

27. Lewis, "Miracles," 5.

28. Lewis, "Miracles," 30.

29. Lewis, *The Screwtape Letters*, 118.

30. Lewis, *Letters to Malcolm*, 93.

5. Fauns Are from Mars, Nymphs Are from Venus

1. Tolkien's comment is discussed in the introduction. See Walter Hooper's editor's note in Lewis, *CL II*, 1041.

2. Letter of July 25, 1916, in *CL I*, 221.

3. Lewis, "Hero and Leander," 60–61.

4. Lewis, *The Discarded Image*, 124–25.

5. Lewis, *The Discarded Image*, 134–35.

6. See Lewis, *The Discarded Image*, 134–38.

7. See Lewis, "Edmund Spenser," 122.

8. Ford, *Companion to Narnia,* 303.

9. Ford, *Companion to Narnia,* 152.

10. Lewis, *The Lion, the Witch and the Wardrobe,* 138.

11. Ford, *Companion to Narnia,* 297.

12. Lewis, *The Lion, the Witch and the Wardrobe,* 138.

13. Lewis, *Prince Caspian,* 52.

14. Lewis, *The Lion, the Witch and the Wardrobe,* 16–17.

15. Lewis, *The Lion, the Witch and the Wardrobe,* 16–17.

16. Lewis, *The Lion, the Witch and the Wardrobe,* 138.

17. Lewis, *Prince Caspian,* 165.

18. Lewis, *The Magician's Nephew,* 198.

19. Lewis, *The Magician's Nephew,* 219.

20. Lewis, *The Last Battle,* 20–21.

21. Most recently in Curtis and Key, eds., *Women and C. S. Lewis.*

22. A verbal club used far too often to beat down dissent—to reject without argument those people, groups, and ideas that the "open minded" and "tolerant" hate and refuse to tolerate.

23. Lewis, "Is Theology Poetry?" 82.

24. Barfield, "Preface," 2.

25. Lewis, "Equality," 666.

26. Lewis, "Equality," 667.

27. "Screwtape Proposes a Toast," in Lewis, *The Screwtape Letters, with Screwtape Proposes a Toast,* 204.

28. Lewis, "Equality," 668.

29. Mitchison, *The Home and a Changing Civilization,* 49–50.

30. Lewis, "Equality," 667–68.

31. Lewis, *That Hideous Strength,* 145.

32. Lewis, *That Hideous Strength,* 146.

33. Lewis, *That Hideous Strength,* 147.

34. Lewis, *That Hideous Strength,* 312.

35. Lewis, *That Hideous Strength,* 212.

36. Lewis, *That Hideous Strength,* 212–13.

37. Lewis, *Perelandra,* 171–72.

38. Lewis, *Perelandra,* 172.

39. Lewis, *That Hideous Strength,* 322.

40. Lewis, *The Pilgrim's Regress,* 54, 56.

41. Lewis, *The Pilgrim's Regress,* 54n. This is David C. Downing's annotation to the passage at hand.

42. Lewis, "Modern Man and His Categories of Thought," 63.

43. Lewis, "Modern Man and His Categories of Thought," 62.

44. For example, Ruth Pitter, Dorothy Sayers, and his wife Joy David-man Gresham.

45. See Lewis, *Mere Christianity*, 96.

46. Lewis, *The Screwtape Letters*, 141–42.

47. Lewis, *Mere Christianity*, 95–96.

48. Lewis, "Priestesses in the Church?" 398.

49. Lewis, "Priestesses in the Church?" 399–400.

50. Lewis, "Priestesses in the Church?" 400.

51. Lewis, "Priestesses in the Church?" 401.

52. Lewis, "Priestesses in the Church?" 402.

53. See, for example, Lewis, *That Hideous Strength*, 151–55, where Hard-castle kidnaps and tortures Jane.

54. See, for example, Lewis, *That Hideous Strength*, 62–66, where she begins to draw Jane into the "company."

55. See Lewis, *That Hideous Strength*, 140–41, 149.

56. Lewis, *The Great Divorce*, 119.

57. Lewis, "A Panegyric for Dorothy Sayers," 570.

58. Lewis, *Miracles*, 143.

59. Lewis, *Miracles*, 145.

60. Lewis, *Miracles*, 148.

61. Lewis, *Miracles*, 149.

62. Lewis, *Miracles*, 152.

63. Lewis, *Miracles*, 153.

64. Lewis, *The Problem of Pain*, 104.

65. Letter of February 5, 1945, in *CL II*, 640.

66. Lewis, *Miracles*, 163.

67. Lewis, *Miracles*, 197.

68. Lewis, *Miracles*, 167.

69. Lewis, *Miracles*, 169.

70. Lewis, *Letters to Malcolm*, 17–18.

71. Also known as "The Magician and the Dryad."

72. Lewis, "Conversation Piece," 366.

73. Lewis, *The Last Battle*, 20–21.

74. Lewis, *Perelandra*, 122.

75. Lewis, *Miracles*, 212.

76. Lewis, "Myth Became Fact," 66.

77. Lewis, "Myth Became Fact," 66.

6. Why Sylvan Myths Matter

1. Lewis, *The Allegory of Love,* 57.
2. Lewis, *The Allegory of Love,* 57–58.
3. See Lewis, *The Allegory of Love,* 57–62.
4. Lewis, *Prince Caspian,* 211–12.
5. Lewis, *Prince Caspian,* 84.
6. Lewis, *Prince Caspian,* 86.
7. Lewis, *Prince Caspian,* 123.
8. Lewis, *Prince Caspian,* 166.
9. Lewis, *Prince Caspian,* 167.
10. Lewis, *Prince Caspian,* 167, 168.
11. Ford, *Companion to Narnia,* 71.
12. Lewis, *Prince Caspian,* 169.
13. Lewis, *Prince Caspian,* 202.
14. Lewis, *Prince Caspian,* 210.
15. Lewis, *Prince Caspian,* 211.
16. Lewis, "Pan's Purge," 342, lines 1–7.
17. Lewis, "Pan's Purge" 343, lines 15–21.
18. Letter of September 26, 1914, in *CL I,* 70.
19. Lewis, *Four Loves,* 29.
20. Lewis, *Four Loves,* 30.
21. See Lewis, *That Hideous Strength,* 169–73.
22. Lewis, *The Lion, the Witch and the Wardrobe,* 98.
23. Lewis, *The Voyage of the Dawn Treader,* 1–2.
24. Letter of April 23, 1935, in *CL II,* 160.
25. Letter of April 23, 1935, in *CL II,* 161.
26. Letter of November 16, 1963, in *CL III,* 1480.
27. Letter of September 20, 1950, in *CL III,* 54.
28. Letter of December 5, 1955, in *CL III,* 677.
29. Letter of October 15, 1947, in *CL II,* 808.
30. Lewis, *Prince Caspian,* 211–12.
31. Lewis, *Prince Caspian,* 214–15.
32. Lewis, *Prince Caspian,* 215.
33. Lewis, *Prince Caspian,* 215–16.
34. Lewis, *Prince Caspian,* 217.
35. Lewis, "The Empty Universe," 81–82.
36. Lewis, *The Voyage of the Dawn Treader,* 226.
37. Luke 19:40 (NIV).
38. See Lewis, *The Silver Chair,* 182–88. For Lewis on wish-fulfillment and other fallacious materialist arguments, see *The Pilgrim's Regress,* 49–67.

39. Lewis, *The Silver Chair*, 190–91.

40. Lewis, *The Silver Chair*, 191.

41. Lewis, "Conversation Piece," 366.

42. Lewis, *The Abolition of Man*, 82.

43. Lewis, "Religion without Dogma?" 101.

44. See Euripides, *Bacchae*, lines 74ff.

45. Lewis, "Religion without Dogma?" 101. See also "A Cliché Came Out of Its Cage," which begins, "You said 'The world is going back to Paganism.' Oh bright / vision!" (375).

46. Wordsworth, "The World is Too Much With Us."

47. Lewis, "The Grand Miracle," 60–61.

48. Lewis, "The Grand Miracle," 60.

49. Lewis, "The Grand Miracle," 57–62.

50. Letter to Arthur Greeves of January 10, 1932, in *CL II*, 35.

51. Lewis, "Song," lines 1–5.

52. Lewis, "Song," lines 19–25.

53. Letter to Greeves of May 29, 1918, in *CL I*, 374.

54. Letter to Sister Penelope of August 24, 1939, in *CL II*, 262.

55. Lewis, "Is Theism Important?" 105. This sentiment is echoed in Lewis's description of Mark Studdock in *That Hideous Strength* who suffers from a complete lack of "noble thought, either Christian or Pagan" because his education had lacked either real scientific or real classical training. It had been merely "Modern" (182).

56. Also known as "The Adam Unparadised."

57. Lewis, "A Footnote to Pre-History," 368, lines 29–35.

58. Lewis, "Is Theology Poetry?" 76.

59. Lewis, *The Pilgrim's Regress*, 204, 201 (for the second definition of Romanticism).

7. Defining Myth

1. Letter to Arthur Greeves of July 4, 1916, in *CL I*, 206.

2. Letter of October 12, 1916, in Lewis, *Letters of C. S. Lewis*, 52.

3. Lewis, "The Satyr," 76, lines 7–10. This is the third poem in Lewis's first book, *Spirits in Bondage;* later in the cycle, a satyr represents a Satan figure.

4. Lewis, "The Satyr," 76, lines 11–13.

5. Lewis, "The Satyr," 76, lines 17–18.

6. Lewis, "The Satyr," 76, lines 21–24.

7. Lewis, "Night," 106, line 29.

8. Letter dated "Whitsunday [May 27, 1928]," in *CL I*, 761.

9. Letter of June [8?], 1928, in *CL I*, 765.

10. Letter of June [8?], 1928, *CL I,* 765.

11. Starr, "Two Pieces from C. S. Lewis's 'Moral Good' Manuscript," 30–62.

12. The original is part of Walter Hooper's personal collection of Lewis manuscripts.

13. This Lewis handwriting chart (LHC) is now available in Starr, "Villainous Handwriting," 73–94.

14. Starr, "Two Pieces from C. S. Lewis's 'Moral Good' Manuscript," 44.

15. Characters from Norse mythology (Atli, based on Attila the Hun) who figure prominently in various versions of the story of Sigurd (or Sigfried), son of Sigmund. Lewis's love for Northern myth is well documented (see especially his autobiography, *Surprised by Joy,* 73–78). We'll look at it near the end of this study.

16. Baron von Richthofen—the German flying ace, who was credited with having shot down eighty allied planes in World War I.

17. This phrase "The origin of myths" appears after "Where do the dragons come from?" but is scratched out in favor of the conclusion that we "must answer that we do not know [the origin of myths]."

18. Starr, "Two Pieces from C. S. Lewis's 'Moral Good' Manuscript," 45.

19. As carefully argued by Lazo, "C. S. Lewis Got It Wrong."

20. Carpenter, *The Inklings,* 146.

21. Carpenter, *The Inklings,* 146n, which reads as follows: "The account of this conversation is based on Tolkien's poem 'Mythopoeia', to which he also gave the titles 'Misomythos' and 'Philomythus to Misomythus'. One manuscript is marked 'For C. S. L.'"

22. Carpenter, *The Inklings,* 146–47.

23. Letter of September 22, 1931, in Lewis, *They Stand Together,* 421.

24. Letter of October 1, 1931, in Lewis, *They Stand Together,* 425.

25. Letter of October 18, 1931, in Lewis, *They Stand Together,* 426.

26. Letter of October 18, 1931, in Lewis, *They Stand Together,* 427.

27. Letter of October 18, 1931, in Lewis, *They Stand Together,* 427–28.

28. Lewis, *Perelandra,* 172.

29. Lewis, "Religion without Dogma?" 87.

30. Lewis, "Religion without Dogma?" 88. An excellent and lengthy parallel can be found in Lewis, *Reflections on the Psalms,* near the end of chapter 10 ("Second Meanings"), 89–91, as well as near the end of chapter 8 ("Nature"), 74, where Lewis discusses Akhenaten. Another parallel is available in Lewis, "Is Theology Poetry?" 78–79.

31. See also a letter to Arthur Greeves of January 10, 1932, in Lewis, *They Stand Together,* 437; *The Problem of Pain,* 25, 103; and *Mere Christianity,* 44.

32. Letter of January 10, 1932, in Lewis, *They Stand Together,* 437.

33. Lewis, *Perelandra*, 173.

34. Lewis, *Miracles*, 176n.

35. See also Lewis's poem "The Sailing of the Ark," also known as "The Late Passenger," in which Noah's son Ham is cursed for failing to open the door to a late arrival—a unicorn.

36. Lewis, *Perelandra*, 88.

37. Letter of June 22, 1930, in *CL I*, 909.

8. Men, Monks, and Gamekeepers; a Study in Popular Legend

1. See Lewis, *The Magician's Nephew*, 116–21.

2. Lewis, "First and Second Things," 653.

3. See, for example, Lewis, "On a Picture by Chirico," "The Turn of the Tide," "Donkey's Delight," "The Small Man Orders His Wedding," and "On the Atomic Bomb (Metrical Experiment)."

4. See, for example, the betrayal of Nikabrik in Lewis, *Prince Caspian*, 171–85.

5. Lewis, *Prince Caspian*, 72.

6. Lewis, "Revival or Decay," 250.

7. Lewis, *The Voyage of the Dawn Treader*, 251.

8. Tolkien, *The Fellowship of the Ring*, 242–43.

9. See, for example, Tolkien, *The Fellowship of the Ring*, 338.

10. Tolkien, *The Two Towers*, 557.

11. Hooper, *Past Watchful Dragons*, 16–17, quoting a Lewis notebook that was given to Walter Hooper by Lewis's brother.

12. Lewis, *An Experiment in Criticism*, 43.

13. Lewis, *An Experiment in Criticism*, 41. See chapter 10 for additional discussion on this topic.

14. Lewis, *An Experiment in Criticism*, 43–44. In the text, all of the quotations related to the six characteristics of myth are from this source.

15. Entry of May 16, 1922, in Lewis, *All My Road before Me*, 35.

16. Letter of September 22, 1956, in Lewis, *Letters of C. S. Lewis*, 458.

17. For the idea that authors can put more meanings in a text than they are aware of, see Lewis's letter of February 20, 1943, in *CL II*, 555. There Lewis argues that any story we make will include elements from creation into which God has already put His meanings; therefore, our stories or other artistic creations will have more meanings in them than we realize.

18. I'll have more to say about myth and meaning in chapter 10.

9. *Is Man a Myth?*

1. See *Prince Caspian,* 101–2, 105–13.
2. Lewis, *The Silver Chair,* 182–89.
3. Lewis, *The Pilgrim's Regress,* 64–66.
4. See Lewis, "The Funeral of a Great Myth," 82–93.
5. Lewis, "The Dethronement of Power," 14–15.
6. Lewis, *The Great Divorce,* 83.
7. See Lewis, *The Pilgrim's Regress,* 210–11; *Surprised by Joy,* 220–21.
8. Lewis, *Mere Christianity,* 115.
9. Lewis, *Miracles,* 177n.
10. Lewis, "The Weight of Glory," 6–7.
11. Lewis, "The Weight of Glory," 11.
12. Lewis, "The Weight of Glory," 11–12.
13. Lewis, "The Weight of Glory," 16.
14. II Corinthians 4:17 (NAS).
15. Lewis, *Perelandra,* 176.
16. See the New American Standard Bible (NAS). Lewis's favorite gospel was John's.
17. Psalm 82:6–7 (NAS).
18. "Passing To-day by a Cottage, I Shed Tears," 235, line 20. This poem is also known as "Scazons."
19. Lewis, *The Problem of Pain,* 42–43.
20. Lewis, "Passing To-day by a Cottage, I Shed Tears," 235, line 20.

10. Mythic Knowing

1. Lucas, *Star Wars: The Empire Strikes Back.*
2. Lewis, "Bluspels and Flalansferes," 265.
3. Lewis, *The Pilgrim's Regress,* 215. See also "Shelley, Dryden, and Mr. Eliot," 29, where Lewis says myth's "primary appeal is to the imagination."
4. Lewis, "The Funeral of a Great Myth," 91.
5. Lewis, "On Science-Fiction," 67.
6. Lewis, *Miracles,* 46.
7. Schakel, *Reason and Imagination in C. S. Lewis,* 183.
8. See Lewis, *Surprised by Joy,* 15–18.
9. Lewis, "The Funeral of a Great Myth," 91.
10. In their recent study, *The Surprising Imagination of C. S. Lewis,* Jerry Root and Mark Neal identify multiple uses or kinds of imagination in the writings of C. S. Lewis, including several that use the imagination to propagate lies and commit and justify sins.

11. In a letter to his brother of April 24, 1928, in *CL I,* 752.

12. In Lewis, "Learning in War-time," 53.

13. In a letter published July 1, 1949, in *CL III,* 1590.

14. In a letter of February 13, 1958, in *CL III,* 920.

15. In a letter of November 26, 1962, in *CL III,* 1384. See also Lewis, *Letters to Malcolm,* 17: "If the imagination were obedient, the appetites would give us very little trouble." And see the letter of June 3, 1956, in which Lewis discusses the dangers of using the imagination for sexual fantasies.

16. Sayers, "'. . . And Telling You a Story': A Note on *The Divine Comedy,*" 32.

17. Lewis, "Religion: Reality or Substitute?" 43.

18. Lewis, *Mere Christianity,* 118.

19. Lewis, *Surprised by Joy,* 167, 167n.

20. Letter of June 3, 1956, in *CL III,* 759.

21. Lewis, *The Screwtape Letters,* 32.

22. Lewis, *The Screwtape Letters,* 31.

23. Lewis, *The Screwtape Letters,* 1–2.

24. See Lewis, *Perelandra,* 107–8, 112–14.

25. In an unpublished letter of September 29, 1956, housed in the Lanier Theological Library, Houston.

26. Lewis, *The Voyage of the Dawn Treader,* 92.

27. Lewis, *The Abolition of Man,* 26–27.

28. Lewis, *An Experiment in Criticism,* 52.

29. Lewis, "Psycho-Analysis and Literary Criticism," 290.

30. Lewis, *An Experiment in Criticism,* 53; "Psycho-Analysis and Literary Criticism," 290.

31. Guite, *Faith, Hope, and Poetry.*

32. Lewis, "Is Theology Poetry?" 75.

33. Lewis, "Is Theology Poetry?" 75.

34. Lewis, "Is Theology Poetry?" 76.

35. Lewis, "Is Theology Poetry?" 76.

36. Lewis, "Horrid Red Things," 44.

37. Lewis, *The Screwtape Letters,* 32.

38. Lewis, "Is Theology Poetry?" 80.

39. Lewis, *Miracles,* 95.

40. Lewis, *Miracles,* 96.

41. Lewis, *Miracles,* 96–97.

42. Lewis, "Is Theology Poetry?" 78–79.

43. Lewis, "Myth Became Fact," 66.

44. Lewis, "Myth Became Fact, "66n.

45. Lewis, "Myth Became Fact," 66. The Latin means "in this valley of separation."

46. Lewis, "The Language of Religion," 138.

47. Lewis, "The Language of Religion," 137.

48. Lewis, "The Language of Religion," 137.

49. Lewis, "The Language of Religion," 140. And see Lewis's letter to Rhona Bodle of June 24, 1949, in *CL II*, 947, on the abstract limitations of language when trying to express the concrete intensity of reality. There, Lewis says that poetry is our attempt to "bring language back to the actual."

50. Lewis, "Myth Became Fact," 66.

51. Lewis, "Myth Became Fact," 65.

52. Lewis, "Myth Became Fact," 66.

53. Lewis, "Myth Became Fact," 66.

54. That is, God Himself, as 1 John 4:8 suggests.

55. Lewis, "Myth Became Fact," 65.

56. See also Tolkien in "On Fairy-Stories," who says, "Something really 'higher' is occasionally glimpsed in mythology," and refers to that *something* as "Divinity" (51).

57. Lewis, "Bluspels and Flalansferes," 265.

58. Lewis, *George MacDonald*, 26–27. See also the parallel passage in chapter 5 of *An Experiment in Criticism*, 41, the fourth paragraph, beginning: "There is, then, a particular kind of story which has a value in itself—a value independent of its embodiment in any literary work."

59. Lewis says something similar in his critique of the fiction of Rider Haggard—that Haggard wasn't a great writer, but he was able to make great myth despite the poor quality of his writing ("The Mythopoeic Gift of Rider Haggard," 98–100).

60. Lewis, *A Preface to Paradise Lost*, 57.

61. Lewis, "On Three Ways of Writing for Children," 27.

62. Lewis, "The Queen of Drum," 282, canto III, lines 21–25.

63. See Lewis's discussion of "pattern of events" (*George MacDonald*, 26–27).

64. Tolkien echoes this idea in his description of dragons: "Dragons always attracted me as a mythological element. They seemed to be able to comprise human malice and bestiality together so extraordinarily well, and also a sort of malicious wisdom and shrewdness—terrifying creatures!" ("BBC Radio Interview" [January 1965], 309n2).

65. See the conclusion to my essay, "The Silver Chair and the Silver Screen," 20.

66. Barfield, *Poetic Diction*, 45–92.

67. Lewis says as much in *Surprised by Joy*, 200.

68. As they enter the "valley of abstraction," described in "Myth Became Fact," 66.

69. Lewis, "The Birth of Language," 25, lines 32, 38.

70. Lewis, *That Hideous Strength,* 281.

71. Lewis, *That Hideous Strength,* 225.

72. Lewis, *That Hideous Strength,* 225–26.

73. Barfield, *Poetic Diction,* 80.

74. See Barfield, *Poetic Diction,* 47–85, for the complete argument.

75. Barfield, *Poetic Diction,* 85.

76. Barfield, *Poetic Diction,* 86.

77. Barfield, *Poetic Diction,* 86–87.

78. Lewis, *English Literature in the Sixteenth Century,* 3–4.

79. Lewis, *Perelandra,* 52.

80. Barfield, *Poetic Diction,* 88.

81. Barfield, *Poetic Diction,* 201.

82. Barfield, *Poetic Diction,* 91.

83. Persephone was taken by Hades to live in the underworld. When her mother, Demeter, an agricultural goddess, went searching for her, the earth fell into an unending winter, and all crops died. Zeus arranged for Persephone's release, but only during certain months of the year—Persephone's "resurrection," or return to the world of the living, occurs in the months of springtime and harvest.

84. Barfield, *Poetic Diction,* 91.

85. Barfield, *Poetic Diction,* 92.

86. Lewis, *The Great Divorce,* 43.

87. Burton and Thompson, *Edward Scissorhands.*

88. Lewis, "The Mythopoeic Gift of Rider Haggard," 100.

11. Lewis and the North

1. See the letter of February 8, 1927, in Lewis, *Letters of C. S. Lewis,* 224.

2. Longfellow, "Tegnér's Drapa," lines 1–3.

3. Lewis, *Surprised by Joy,* 17.

4. Lewis, *Surprised by Joy,* 78.

5. Lewis, *Surprised by Joy,* 211 (and see also page 77 for additional context).

6. Letter of February 8, 1927, in Lewis, *Letters of C. S. Lewis,* 224.

7. An Internet search for the book title plus the artist's name will allow you to see the series of illustrations Rackham made for the book. They're stunning.

8. Lewis, *Surprised by Joy,* 73.

9. Lewis, *Surprised by Joy*, 76–77.

10. Lewis, *Surprised by Joy*, 82.

11. For this incomplete poem, see Lewis, "Descend to Earth, Descend, Celestial Nine."

12. Lewis, *Surprised by Joy*, 74.

13. See *CL I*, 75–78, and the letter of October 14, 1914, in *CL I*, 80–81.

14. See Lewis, "Loki Bound." Lewis wrote another, much shorter Norse poem in 1929, "Artless and Ignorant Is Andvari," which has parallels with the "Celestial Nine" poem. Lewis comments on the significance of "Loki Bound" in regard to his intellectual journey in *Surprised by Joy*, 114–15. One more poetic reference to Norse mythology appears in the form of the epigram to Lewis's 1926 narrative poem "Dymer" (which he began working on in 1916). There he quotes from the *Poetic Edda*, where Odin says he hung upon the great ash tree Yggdrasil for nine nights "as an offering to / Odin, myself sacrificed to myself" (see Lewis, "Dymer," 148). Additionally, Lewis worked on a version of "Dymer" that, for a while, changed the hero's name from Dymer to "Ask," which is the name of a character from Norse mythology (according to the letter of December 2, 1918, in *CL I*, 419).

15. Lewis, *Surprised by Joy*, 77–78.

16. Lewis, *Surprised by Joy*, 130.

17. Lewis, *Surprised by Joy*, 165.

18. See Sayer, *Jack*, 194, 249.

19. In a letter of June 26, 1927, in *They Stand Together*, 298.

20. In a letter from Tolkien to Clyde Kilby of December 18, 1965, in *The Letters of J. R. R. Tolkien*, 366; also see Lewis's letter of September 23, 1963, in *CL III*, 1458.

21. In a letter of September 23, 1963, in *CL III*, 1458.

22. See Sayer, *Jack*, 249.

23. See Lewis, "First and Second Things," 653–54.

24. Lewis, "Historicism," 103.

25. Lewis, *The Lion, the Witch and the Wardrobe*, 64.

26. For the American edition, see Lewis, *The Lion, the Witch and the Wardrobe* (New York: Macmillan, 1950), 55.

27. See Ford, *Companion to Narnia*, 189.

28. Lewis, *The Lion, the Witch and the Wardrobe*, 155.

29. For the American edition, see Lewis, *The Lion, the Witch and the Wardrobe* (New York: Macmillan, 1950), 138.

30. See Ford, *Companion to Narnia*, 447.

31. This idea, by the way, is echoed in Lewis, "First and Second Things."

32. See Starr, "Two Pieces from C. S. Lewis's 'Moral Good' Manuscript," 44, 57n25.

33. For the complete story, see Poe, "C. S. Lewis Was a Secret Government Agent."

34. Lewis, "Foreword to Joy Davidman, *Smoke on the Mountain*," 178.

35. "Lewis, "Foreword to Joy Davidman, *Smoke on the Mountain*," 179. See also stanza two of Lewis, "A Cliché Came Out of Its Cage," 398–99.

12. An Interpretive Mystery of Mythic Proportion

1. Lewis, "Early Prose Joy," 5–49.

2. Lewis, "Early Prose Joy," 39–40 (emphasis added).

3. Lewis, *The Pilgrim's Regress*, 174.

4. Lewis, "Myth Became Fact," 66 (emphasis added).

5. I actually wrote my doctoral dissertation on fact, truth, and myth in Lewis's epistemological thinking.

6. For those interested in exploring this puzzle more fully, I want to recommend the following resources: In *Reason and Imagination in C. S. Lewis,* esp. 123–24, Schakel offered an early explanation of these problematic passages. Schakel's basic argument is that Lewis's ideas on myth evolved over the years (but that's an oversimplification). In *Joy and Poetic Imagination,* esp. 154n17, Thorson offers some significant information on Lewis's epistemology and deals with the contradiction (focusing on *The Pilgrim's Regress* and "Myth Became Fact"). Thorson suggests the underlying meaning of both texts is essentially the same, and a shift in vocabulary makes for the apparent contradiction. Then there are some key Lewis passages on myth to consider, most of which have been discussed in this book but have not been quoted in their entirety. It's a good idea to read all of "Myth Became Fact," the entire text of "Early Prose Joy" (or at least the last three pages), and the relevant chapter in *The Pilgrim's Regress* (Book IX, chapter 5, "Across the Canyon") so you can see the contexts in which our troubling texts are set. In addition, I recommend reading the entirety of Lewis's key footnote on myth in *Miracles* (it's in chapter 11) and all of "Is Theology Poetry?" Finally, there is the letter of October 18, 1931, that Lewis wrote to Arthur Greeves, in which he explains how the new understanding of myth that came to him after talking to Tolkien and Dyson contributed to his conversion to Christianity. We examined portions of this letter in chapter 7.

7. It may be, for example, that *it* refers to God's revelation in the Bible. Another minor theme in Lewis and myth, which has not really been addressed in this book, is Lewis's belief that portions of scripture are mythic (and therefore still true), but not historical. He explains this in the above-mentioned *Miracles* footnote and elsewhere. I've relegated

this topic to a footnote because to spend more time on it would require diving into Lewis's theology of scripture, and that would take us too far from a study of myth.

8. Lewis, *Perelandra,* 122.

9. Lewis, "Early Prose Joy," 39.

10. Notice that Lewis's thoughts are given in "Early Prose Joy" in the context of prayer. A confirmation of the direction I'm taking here can be found in Lewis's poem "He Whom I Bow To," also called "Footnote to All Prayers," in which Lewis expresses to God his realization that whatever he prays will in some sense be blasphemous because Lewis's own conception of God will always fall short of who He really is. This is significant because—by using my Lewis Handwriting Chart (Starr, "Villainous Handwriting," 73–94), along with Andrew Lazo's June 1930 date for Lewis's theistic conversion—I can confirm that this poem was written almost immediately after Lewis's conversion to theism. The hesitation Lewis expresses on praying to God in "Early Prose Joy" is the same hesitation he expresses in "He Whom I Bow To." This makes sense if both are written about Lewis's thoughts right at his conversion to theism.

11. Semele saw the true essence of Zeus in all his glory and was consumed by it.

12. Lewis, "Early Prose Joy," 39–40. *The Pilgrim's Regress* offers a similar follow-up to the key myth statement.

13. Lewis is almost certainly suggesting this same idea in a letter of April 24, [1936], in *CL II,* 189, where he notes that the Hebrew Bible carries us to the highest of religious understandings prior to Christianity, while also being as "anthropomorphic" as many pagan religions. Then Lewis notes that this "anthropomorphism" was the thing that had held him so long from belief and that what he thought had been philosophical honesty on his part had really turned out to be a form of pride.

14. Letter of October 18, 1931, in Lewis, *Letters of C. S. Lewis,* 289.

Bibliography

Barfield, Owen. *Poetic Diction: A Study in Meaning*. 1928. Middletown, Conn.: Wesleyan Univ. Press, 1973.

——. "Preface." In *The Taste of the Pineapple: Essays on C. S. Lewis as a Reader, Critic, and Imaginative Writer*, edited by Bruce Edwards, 1-2. Bowling Green, Ohio: Bowling Green State Univ. Press, 1988.

Burton, Tim, and Caroline Thompson. *Edward Scissorhands*, directed by Tim Burton. Los Angeles: Twentieth Century Fox, 1990.

Campbell, Joseph. *The Hero with a Thousand Faces*. New York: Pantheon Books, 1949.

Carpenter, Humphrey. *The Inklings: C. S. Lewis, J. R. R. Tolkien, Charles Williams, and Their Friends*. London: George Allen and Unwin, 1978.

Christopher, Joe R. "C. S. Lewis's Two Satyrs." *Mythlore* 34, no. 2 (Spring/Summer 2016): 83-93.

Curtis, Carolyn, and Mary Pomroy Key, eds. *Women and C. S. Lewis: What His Life and Literature Reveal for Today's Culture*. Oxford: Lion Hudson, 2015.

Dickieson, Brenton. "The Unpublished Preface to C. S. Lewis' *The Screwtape Letters*." *Notes and Queries* 2 (2013): 296-98.

Ford, Paul. *Companion to Narnia*. New York: Macmillan, 1986.

Frye, Northrop. *Anatomy of Criticism: Four Essays*. Princeton, N.J.: Princeton Univ. Press, 1957.

Guite, Malcolm. *Faith, Hope, and Poetry: Theology and the Poetic Imagination*. Farnham, Surrey: Ashgate, 2012.

Holy Bible, New American Standard Bible (NAS). LaHabra, Calif.: Lockman Foundation, 1995.

Holy Bible, New International Version (NIV). Grand Rapids, Mich.: Zondervan Publishing House, 2011.

Hooper, Walter. *Past Watchful Dragons: The Narnia Chronicles of C. S. Lewis*. New York: Collier, 1979.

Lazo, Andrew. "C. S. Lewis Got It Wrong: A Reliable Date for Theistic Conversion." *First Things.* August 8, 2013. https://www.firstthings.com/web-exclusives/2013/08/c-s-lewis-got-it-wrong.

Lewis, C. S. *The Abolition of Man.* New York: Collier, 1955.

———. *The Allegory of Love: A Study in Medieval Tradition.* 1936. Oxford: Oxford Univ. Press, 1958.

———. *All My Road before Me: The Diary of C. S. Lewis, 1922–1927,* edited by Walter Hooper. San Diego: Harvest/HBJ, 1991.

———. "Artless and Ignorant Is Andvari." In *The Collected Poems of C. S. Lewis: A Critical Edition,* edited by Don W. King, 222. Kent, Ohio: Kent State Univ. Press, 2015.

———. "The Birth of Language." In *The Collected Poems of C. S. Lewis: A Critical Edition,* edited by Don W. King, 337–38. Kent, Ohio: Kent State Univ. Press.

———. "Bluspels and Flalansferes: A Semantic Nightmare." In *Selected Literary Essays,* edited by Walter Hooper, 251–65. Cambridge: Cambridge Univ. Press, 1969.

———. "Bulverism." In *The Socratic Digest,* edited by Joel Heck, 42–45. Austin, Tex.: Concordia Univ. Press, 2012.

———. "A Cliché Came Out of Its Cage." In *The Collected Poems of C. S. Lewis: A Critical Edition,* edited by Don W. King, 375–76. Kent, Ohio: Kent State Univ. Press, 2015.

———. *The Collected Letters of C. S. Lewis.* Vol. 2, *Books, Broadcasts, and the War, 1931–1949,* edited by Walter Hooper. San Francisco: Harper Collins, 2004.

———. *The Collected Letters of C. S. Lewis.* Vol. 1, *Family Letters, 1905–1931,* edited by Walter Hooper. London: Harper Collins, 2000.

———. *The Collected Letters of C. S. Lewis.* Vol. 3, *Narnia, Cambridge, and Joy, 1950–1963,* edited by Walter Hooper. London: Harper Collins, 2007.

———. *The Collected Poems of C. S. Lewis: A Critical Edition,* edited by Walter Hooper. London: Fount, 1994.

———. "Commentary on LEWIS Ad Familiares Epist XXXVII." Unpublished portion of a letter from Lewis to Owen Barfield, dated March 22, 1932. CSL/L-Barfield 28. Marion E. Wade Center, Wheaton College.

———. "Commentary on *The Lay of Leithian.*" In *The History of Middle-earth;* vol. 3, *The Lays of Beleriand,* by J. R. R. Tolkien, edited by Christopher Tolkien, 184–85 and 374–92. New York: Ballantine, 1985.

———. "Conversation Piece." In *The Collected Poems of C. S. Lewis: A Critical Edition,* edited by Don W. King, 366–67. Kent, Ohio: Kent State Univ. Press, 2015.

———. "The Dark Tower." In *The Dark Tower and Other Stories,* edited by Walter Hooper, 15–98. San Diego: Harcourt Brace, 1977.

———. "Descend to Earth, Descend, Celestial Nine." In *The Collected Poems of C. S. Lewis: A Critical Edition*, edited by Don W. King, 10–29. Kent, Ohio: Kent State Univ. Press, 2015.

———. "The Dethronement of Power." In *Understanding* The Lord of the Rings: *The Best of Tolkien Criticism*, edited by Rose A. Zimbardo and Neil D. Isaacs, 11–15. Boston: Houghton Mifflin, 2004.

———. *The Discarded Image: An Introduction to Medieval and Renaissance Literature.* Cambridge: Cambridge Univ. Press, 1964.

———. "Donkey's Delight." In *The Collected Poems of C. S. Lewis: A Critical Edition,* edited by Don W. King, 350. Kent, Ohio: Kent State Univ. Press, 2015.

———. "Dymer." In *The Collected Poems of C. S. Lewis: A Critical Edition*, edited by Don W. King, 144–215. Kent, Ohio: Kent State Univ. Press, 2015.

———. "'Early Prose Joy': C. S. Lewis's Early Draft of an Autobiographical Manuscript," edited by Andrew Lazo. *VII: An Anglo-American Literary Review* 30 (2013): 13–49.

———. "Edmund Spenser." In *Studies in Medieval and Renaissance Literature*, edited by Walter Hooper, 121–45. Cambridge: Cambridge Univ. Press, 1966.

———. "The Empty Universe." In *Present Concerns: Essays by C. S. Lewis,* edited by Walter Hooper, 81–86. San Diego: HBJ, 1986.

———. *English Literature in the Sixteenth Century, Excluding Drama.* Oxford History of English Literature 3. Oxford: Clarendon, 1954.

———. "Equality." In *Essay Collection and Other Short Pieces,* edited by Lesley Walmsley, 666–68. London: HarperCollins, 2000.

———. *An Experiment in Criticism.* Cambridge: Cambridge Univ. Press, 1961.

———. "Fern-seed and Elephants." In *Fern-seed and Elephants and Other Essays on Christianity,* edited by Walter Hooper, 104–25. Glasgow: Fontana/Collins, 1975.

———. "First and Second Things." In *Essay Collection and Other Short Pieces,* edited by Lesley Walmsley, 653–56. London: HarperCollins, 2000.

———. "A Footnote to Pre-History." In *The Collected Poems of C. S. Lewis: A Critical Edition,* edited by Don W. King, 368–69. Kent, Ohio: Kent State Univ. Press, 2015.

———. "Foreword to Joy Davidman, *Smoke on the Mountain: An Interpretation of the Ten Commandments.*" In *Image and Imagination: Essays and Reviews,* edited by Walter Hooper, 174–80. Cambridge: Cambridge Univ. Press, 2013.

———. "Forms of Things Unknown." In *The Dark Tower and Other Stories,* edited by Walter Hooper, 124–32. San Diego: Harcourt Brace, 1977.

———. *The Four Loves.* San Diego: Harvest/HBJ, 1960.

———. "From Johnson's *Life of Fox.*" *The Oxford Magazine* (June 9, 1938): 737–38.

———. "The Funeral of a Great Myth." In *Christian Reflections,* edited by Walter Hooper, 82–93. Grand Rapids, Mich.: Eerdmans, 1967.

———, ed. *George MacDonald: An Anthology.* London: Fount Paperbacks, 1946.

———. "The Grand Miracle." In *The Grand Miracle and Other Selected Essays on Theology and Ethics from* God in the Dock, edited by Walter Hooper, 55–62. New York: Ballantine, 1970.

———. *The Great Divorce.* San Francisco: HarperCollins, 1973.

———. *A Grief Observed.* San Francisco: HarperCollins, 1989.

———. "Hamlet: The Prince or the Poem?" In *Selected Literary Essays,* edited by Walter Hooper, 88–105. Cambridge: Cambridge Univ. Press, 1969.

———. "He Whom I Bow To." In *The Collected Poems of C. S. Lewis: A Critical Edition,* edited by Don W. King, 225. Kent, Ohio: Kent State Univ. Press, 2015.

———. "Hero and Leander." In *Selected Literary Essays,* edited by Walter Hooper, 58–73. Cambridge: Cambridge Univ. Press, 1969.

———. "Historicism." In *Christian Reflections,* edited by Walter Hooper, 100–113. Grand Rapids, Mich.: Eerdmans, 1967.

———. "The Hobbit." In *On Stories and Other Essays on Literature,* edited by Walter Hooper, 81–82. San Diego: Harvest/HBJ, 1982.

———. "Horrid Red Things." In *The Grand Miracle and Other Essays on Theology and Ethics from* God in the Dock, edited by Walter Hooper, 43–46. New York: Ballantine, 1970.

———. *The Horse and His Boy.* New York: HarperCollins, 1954.

———. "Is Theism Important?" In *Timeless at Heart: Essays on Theology,* edited by Walter Hooper, 105–9. London: Fount, 1987.

———. "Is Theology Poetry?" In *The Socratic Digest,* edited by Joel Heck, 75–82. Austin, Tex.: Concordia Univ. Press, 2012.

———. "It All Began with a Picture." In *Of Other Worlds: Essays and Stories,* edited by Walter Hooper, 42. New York: Harvest/HBJ, 1966.

———. "The Language of Religion." In *Christian Reflections,* edited by Walter Hooper, 129–41. Grand Rapids, Mich.: Eerdmans, 1967.

———. *The Last Battle.* New York: HarperCollins, 1956.

———. "Learning in War-time." In *Transposition and Other Addresses,* 45–54. London: Geoffrey Bles, 1949.

———. *Letters of C. S. Lewis: Revised and Enlarged Edition,* edited by W. H. Lewis. Rev. ed., edited by Walter Hooper. 1966. San Diego: Harvest/HBJ, 1993.

———. *Letters to Malcolm: Chiefly on Prayer.* San Diego: Harvest/HBJ, 1964.

———. *The Lion, the Witch and the Wardrobe.* New York: HarperCollins, 1950.

———. "Loki Bound." In *The Collected Poems of C. S. Lewis: A Critical Edition,* edited by Don W. King, 33–36. Kent, Ohio: Kent State Univ. Press, 2015.

———. *The Magician's Nephew.* New York: HarperCollins, 1955.

———. *Mere Christianity.* Christian Library. Westwood, N.J.: Barbour and Company, 1952.

———. *Miracles: A Preliminary Study.* New York: Touchstone, 1975.

———. "Miracles." In *The Grand Miracle and Other Selected Essays on Theology and Ethics from* God in the Dock, edited by Walter Hooper, 1–13. New York: Ballantine, 1970.

———. "Modern Man and His Categories of Thought." In *Present Concerns: Essays by C. S. Lewis,* edited by Walter Hooper, 61–66. San Diego: Harvest/HBJ, 1986.

———. "Myth Became Fact." In *God in the Dock: Essays on Theology and Ethics,* edited by Walter Hooper, 63–67. Grand Rapids: Eerdmans, 1970.

———. "Mythonomy." In "Two Pieces from C. S. Lewis's 'Moral Good' Manuscript: A First Publication." *VII: An Anglo-American Literary Review* 31 (2014): 30–62.

———. "The Mythopoeic Gift of Rider Haggard." In *On Stories and Other Essays on Literature,* edited by Walter Hooper, 97–100. San Diego: Harvest/HBJ, 1982.

———. "Night." In *The Collected Poems of C. S. Lewis: A Critical Edition,* edited by Don W. King, 105–6. Kent, Ohio: Kent State Univ. Press, 2015.

———. "On a Picture by Chirico." In *The Collected Poems of C. S. Lewis: A Critical Edition,* edited by Don W. King, 362. Kent, Ohio: Kent State Univ. Press, 2015.

———. "On Science-Fiction." In *On Stories and Other Essays on Literature,* edited by Walter Hooper, 55–68. San Diego: Harvest/HBJ, 1982.

———. "On the Atomic Bomb (Metrical Experiment)." In *The Collected Poems of C. S. Lewis: A Critical Edition,* edited by Don W. King, 335–36. Kent, Ohio: Kent State Univ. Press, 2015.

———. "On Three Ways of Writing for Children." In *Of Other Worlds: Essays and Stories,* edited by Walter Hooper, 22–34. New York: Harvest/HBJ, 1966.

———. *Out of the Silent Planet.* New York: Scribner, 2003.

———. "A Panegyric for Dorothy Sayers." In *Essay Collection and Other Short Pieces,* edited by Lesley Walmsley, 567–70. London: HarperCollins, 2000.

———. "Pan's Purge." In *The Collected Poems of C. S. Lewis: A Critical Edition,* edited by Don W. King, 342–43. Kent, Ohio: Kent State Univ. Press, 2015.

———. "Passing To-day by a Cottage, I Shed Tears." In *The Collected Poems of C. S. Lewis: A Critical Edition,* edited by Don W. King, 235. Kent, Ohio: Kent State Univ. Press, 2015.

——. *Perelandra.* New York: Scribner, 2003.

——. "Period Criticism." In *Essay Collection and Other Short Pieces,* edited by Lesley Walmsley, 487–90. London: HarperCollins, 2000.

——. *The Pilgrim's Regress: Wade Annotated Edition.* Edited by David C. Downing. Grand Rapids, Mich.: Eerdmans, 2014.

——. *A Preface to Paradise Lost.* London: Oxford Univ. Press, 1961.

——. "Priestesses in the Church?" In *Essay Collection and Other Short Pieces,* edited by Lesley Walmsley, 398–402. London: HarperCollins, 2000.

——. *Prince Caspian: The Return to Narnia.* New York: HarperCollins, 1951.

——. *The Problem of Pain.* New York: Macmillan, 1940.

——. "The Psalms." In *Christian Reflections,* edited by Walter Hooper, 114–28. Grand Rapids, Mich.: Eerdmans, 1967.

——. "Psycho-Analysis and Literary Criticism." In *Selected Literary Essays,* edited by Walter Hooper, 286–300. Cambridge: Cambridge Univ. Press, 1969.

——. "The Queen of Drum." In *The Collected Poems of C. S. Lewis: A Critical Edition,* edited by Don W. King, 268–304. Kent, Ohio: Kent State Univ. Press, 2015.

——. *Reflections on the Psalms.* London: Fontana, 1958.

——. "Religion: Reality or Substitute?" In *Christian Reflections,* edited by Walter Hooper, 37–43. Grand Rapids, Mich.: Eerdmans, 1967.

——. "Religion and Rocketry." In *The World's Last Night and Other Essays,* 83–92. San Diego: Harcourt, Brace, 1987.

——. "Religion without Dogma?" In *Timeless at Heart: Essays on Theology,* edited by Walter Hooper, 84–104. London: Fount, 1987.

——. "Revival or Decay." *God in the Dock: Essays on Theology and Ethics,* edited by Walter Hooper, 250–53. Grand Rapids, Mich.: Eerdmans, 1970.

——. "The Sailing of the Ark." In *The Collected Poems of C. S. Lewis: A Critical Edition,* edited by Don W. King, 355–56. Kent, Ohio: Kent State Univ. Press, 2015.

——. "The Satyr." In *The Collected Poems of C. S. Lewis: A Critical Edition,* edited by Don W. King, 76. Kent, Ohio: Kent State Univ. Press, 2015.

——. *The Screwtape Letters, with Screwtape Proposes a Toast.* San Francisco: HarperCollins, 1996.

——. "Shelley, Dryden, and Mr. Eliot." In *Selected Literary Essays,* edited by Walter Hooper, 187–208. Cambridge: Cambridge Univ. Press, 1969.

——. *The Silver Chair.* New York: HarperCollins, 1953.

——. "The Small Man Orders His Wedding" In *The Collected Poems of C. S. Lewis: A Critical Edition,* edited by Don W. King, 346–47. Kent, Ohio: Kent State Univ. Press, 2015.

——. "Sometimes Fairy Stories May Say Best What's To Be Said." In *Of*

Other Worlds: Essays and Stories, edited by Walter Hooper, 35–38. New York: Harvest/HBJ, 1966.

———. "Song." In *The Collected Poems of C. S. Lewis: A Critical Edition,* edited by Don W. King, 102–3. Kent, Ohio: Kent State Univ. Press, 2015.

———. *Spenser's Images of Life.* Cambridge: Cambridge Univ. Press, 1967.

———. *Surprised by Joy: The Shape of My Early Life.* San Diego: Harvest/ HBJ, 1955.

———. *That Hideous Strength.* New York: Scribner, 2003.

———. *They Stand Together: The Letters of C. S. Lewis to Arthur Greeves (1914– 1963),* edited by Walter Hooper. New York: Macmillan, 1979.

———. *Till We Have Faces: A Myth Retold.* San Diego: Harcourt Brace, 1985.

———. "Tolkien's *The Lord of the Rings.*" In *On Stories and Other Essays on Literature,* edited by Walter Hooper, 83–90. San Diego: Harvest/HBJ, 1982.

———. "The Turn of the Tide." In *The Collected Poems of C. S. Lewis: A Critical Edition,* edited by Don W. King, 358–60. Kent, Ohio: Kent State Univ. Press, 2015.

———. Unpublished letter of September 29, 1956. C. S. Lewis Collection, Lanier Theological Library, Houston.

———. *The Voyage of the Dawn Treader.* New York: HarperCollins, 1952.

———. "The Weight of Glory." In *The Weight of Glory and Other Addresses,* edited by Walter Hooper, 3–19. New York: Macmillan, 1980.

———. "Xmas and Christmas." In *God in the Dock: Essays on Theology and Ethics,* edited by Walter Hooper, 301–3. Grand Rapids, Mich.: Eerdmans, 1970.

Longfellow, Henry Wadsworth. "Tegnér's Drapa." Open source. http:// www.hwlongfellow.org/poems_poem.php?pid=124.

Lucas, George. *Star Wars: A New Hope,* directed by George Lucas. Los Angeles: 20th Century Fox, 1977.

———. *Star Wars: The Empire Strikes Back,* directed by Irvin Kershner. Los Angeles: 20th Century Fox, 1980.

Mead, Marjorie Lamp. "*Letters to Malcolm:* C. S. Lewis on Prayer." In *C. S. Lewis: Life, Works, and Legacy;* vol. 3, *Apologist, Philosopher, and Theologian,* edited by Bruce L. Edwards, 209–35. London: Praeger, 2007.

Mitchison, Naomi. *The Home and a Changing Civilization.* London: 1934.

Morford, Mark P. O., and Robert J. Lenardon. *Classical Mythology.* London: Longman, 1985.

Myers, Doris T. "Browsing the Glome Library." *VII: An Anglo-American Literary Review* 19 (2002).

Poe, Harry Lee. "C. S. Lewis Was a Secret Government Agent." *Christianity Today* 10 (December 2015). http://www.christianitytoday.com/ct /2015/december-web-only/cs-lewis-secret-agent.html.

Root, Jerry, and Mark Neal. *The Surprising Imagination of C. S. Lewis: An Introduction*. Nashville, Tenn.: Abingdon Press, 2015.

Sayer, George. *Jack: A Life of C. S. Lewis*. Wheaton, Ill.: Crossway Books, 1994.

Sayers, Dorothy. "'. . . And Telling You a Story': A Note on *The Divine Comedy*." In *Essays Presented to Charles Williams*, 1–37. Grand Rapids, Mich.: Eerdmans, 1966.

Schakel, Peter. *Imagination and the Arts in C. S. Lewis*. Columbia: Univ. of Missouri Press, 2002.

———. *Reason and Imagination in C. S. Lewis: A Study of Till We Have Faces*. Grand Rapids, Mich.: Eerdmans, 1984.

Seabrook, John. "Why Is the Force Still with Us?" *The New Yorker* (January 6, 1997). http://www.newyorker.com/magazine/1997/01/06/why-is -the-force-still-with-us.

Shippey, Tom. *J. R. R. Tolkien: Author of the Century*. Boston: Houghton Mifflin, 2000.

Sophocles. *Ichneutai* [The Searching Satyrs]. In *Two Satyr Plays: Euripides' Cyclops and Sophocles' Ichneutai*, translated by Roger Lancelyn Green. New York: Penguin, 1957.

Starr, Charlie W. "The Silver Chair and the Silver Screen." In *Revisiting Narnia: Myth and Religion in C. S. Lewis' Chronicles*, edited by Shanna Caughey, 3–23. Dallas: BenBella Books, 2005.

———. "Two Pieces from C. S. Lewis's 'Moral Good' Manuscript: A First Publication." *VII: An Anglo-American Literary Review* 31 (2014): 30–62.

———. "'Villainous Handwriting': A Chronological Study of C. S. Lewis's Script." *VII: Journal of the Marion E. Wade Center* 33 (2016): 73–94.

Thorson, Stephen. *Joy and Poetic Imagination: Understanding C. S. Lewis's "Great War" with Owen Barfield and Its Significance for Lewis's Conversion and Writings*. Hamden, Conn.: Winged Lion, 2015.

Tolkien, J. R. R. "BBC Radio Interview" (January 1965). Quoted in *The Annotated Hobbit*, edited by Douglas A. Anderson, 309n2. Boston: Houghton Mifflin Harcourt, 2002.

———. *The Fellowship of the Ring: Being the First Part of* The Lord of the Rings. Boston: Houghton Mifflin, 1994.

———. *The Letters of J. R. R. Tolkien*, edited by Humphrey Carpenter. Boston: Houghton Mifflin, 1981.

———. "Mythopoeia." In *Tree and Leaf*, 83–90. London: HarperCollins, 2001.

———. "On Fairy-Stories." In *The Tolkien Reader*, 33–99. New York: Ballantine Books, 1966.

———. *The Silmarillion*, edited by Christopher Tolkien. New York: Ballantine Books, 1977.

———. *The Two Towers: Being the Second Part of The Lord of the Rings.* Boston: Houghton Mifflin, 1994.

Wagner, Richard. *Siegfried and the Twilight of the Gods.* Illustrated by Arthur Rackham. London: William Heinemann, 1911.

Wordsworth, William. "The World is Too Much with Us." Open source. https://www.poetryfoundation.org/poems/45564/the-world-is-too-much-with-us.

Index

equality, problems with, 39–41
"Equality" (Lewis), 40
ethics, 24, 108
Euhemerus, 77
Euripides, 30
Eurydice, 14, 114
Eustace, x, xi, xii, 6, 59, 62, 63
Eve, 52, 82, 107; Adam and, 22, 66, 79, 96, 121
evil, 49, 71, 107
Exorcist, The (film), xix
experience, 53, 102, 105, 116, 120; concrete, 115; mythic, ix, x, 87, 104, 112; spiritual, 117; thinking and, 113, 114
Experiment in Criticism, An (Lewis), 86, 108, 157n58

fact, 160n5; myth and, 53, 54, 109, 136, 140; proposition about, 112; reality and, 137; truth and, 136
Faerie Queene (Spenser), 17
faeries, 38, 56, 65
fairy tales, 91, 94
faith, 35, 84; imagination and, 105
Faith, Hope, and Poetry (Guite), 108
Fall, 53, 79, 119, 124
Fantasia (Disney), 29
fantastic literature, 87, 127
faun-catchers, 82
faunettes, 39
fauns, 14, 17, 18, 57, 140; bookshelf of, xviii, 69, 99; dryads and, 121; dwarves and, 13; faeries and, 56; imagination and, 54; masculine reality and, 52; nymphs and, 16, 37, 38, 39, 51, 54
Faunus, 14, 17
feelings, objects and, 120
Fellowship of the Rings, The (Tolkien), 10, 11
feminine, 47, 48; masculine and, 42, 43, 44, 45, 46
feminism, 39, 45, 47
"Fern-seed and Elephants" (Lewis), 6
fiction, xviii, xix, 73; fictitious books of, 3–10
figurative, literal and, 119
film, myth and, 123, 124
Firor, Warfield, 146n35

"First and Second Things" (Lewis), 83, 131
"Footnote to All Prayers" (Lewis), 161n10
"Footnote to Prehistory, A" (Lewis), 66, 79
Ford, Paul, 13–14, 143n3
"Forms of Things Unknown" (Lewis), 21
Fox, Adam, 8
Frank, King, 38
Freud, Sigmund, 41, 91
Frodo, 85
Frye, Northrop, 10
"Funeral of a Great Myth, The" (Lewis), 91

Gaius, 8
gamekeepers, 82–83
Garden of the Hesperides, 22
gender, 50, 97; complexity of, 41, 48; differences in, 45; incarnation and, 38–48; physical, 42, 45, 48; questions related to, 39; sexual differentiation and, 44; as social construct, 44; spiritual, 42, 43, 44, 45, 47, 48, 51; sylvans and, 51, 52; theory of, 42, 43; transcendent, 45
Genesis, 12, 39
ghost: Episcopal, 7; fear of, 50
giants, 66, 81
Glome Library, 7
glory, 32, 93, 96
Gnosticism, 49
God, 23–24, 54, 146n16; Adam and, 12; bright footprints of, 66; Christianity and, 77, 139; Incarnation and, 49; Jesus and, 113; Moses and, 31; myth and, 77, 139; nature of, 138; pagan peoples and, 24; as priest, 47; rejection of, 91; super-personal life of, 15; Trinitarian nature of, 15; woman and, 46
goddesses, 96; priestesses and, 47
Godfather, The (film), xix
gods, 96, 97; nature of, 49; Norse, 128, 129; pagan, 56, 57, 66, 109; as symbols, 55
Gondor, 85
Graal, 65